THE FINANCIAL FITNE$$ HANDBOOK:

Making Your Money Outlast You

 **Checklists for Achieving Peace of Mind About Your Financial Future**

By

LOUIS BERLIN, C.E.O.

For Men and Women of All Ages and Incomes

BERLIN CONSULTING GROUP
www.InsuranceForEnchancedLiving.com

ISBN: 0615501907
ISBN-13: 9780615501901

TABLE OF CONTENTS

LIST 7: Eight Rules for Preparing for the Future (Financial Security in Retirement)..67

INTRODUCTION: THE SINGLE MOST IMPORTANT FINANCIAL RULE (THE FINANCIAL "GOLDEN RULE")

You have two choices, and only two choices, when it comes to your financial future.

You can either let your finances control you, or you can take control and plan, manage, adjust and direct how much money you have, how much money you earn, and how much money you have to spend.

Most people opt for the first choice. Here are the reasons they give:

"I don't make enough money to save anything."

"I have a retirement plan at work—I'm sure I'll be okay."

"Social Security will take care of me."

"I'll probably just keep working until I die."

"My accountant is looking after all of that." (or brother-in-law, financial planner, or husband, etc.)

"I've put some money in some mutual funds, and that should be okay."

"Worst comes to worst, I'll go live with my kids."

"I expect to be getting a nice piece of change when (name a relative) dies."

Here's the reason they never give:

"Figuring out my options for my financial future is a huge and complex task. I don't understand a lot of what I read in the business section of the newspaper, or in the direct mail ads I keep getting. There are lots of choices, and I don't know who to trust. Everything sounds great, but it seems like everyone who is trying to sell me anything is going to make a lot of money if I buy, and I have no way of knowing if I've done the right thing."

That's why I wrote this book.

Mapping out your financial future **is** a huge and complex task, if you look at the whole thing at once. But you can break it out into small, discreet, and understandable pieces.

A lot of what you read **is** designed to confuse you. People use strange terms, and wave numbers around without explaining how they got there, what they mean, and how you can check to see if they are accurate.

There **are** a lot of choices. This is a good thing—there are some real gems among them, and it is not that hard to find them, and figure out if they are appropriate for you.

You **do** know who to trust. That person is you. You've been able to manage your life this far, become successful at what you do, and have gotten yourself to the point where you realize that you need to take control of your financial future, and not the other way around. You know that you are not willing to let circumstances, the economy, your job, the market, or things that happen determine how comfortable you will be financially for the rest of your life. You are bright. The problem is, you are unfamiliar with, or uneducated about, a lot of the possibilities you have, and the merits, and risks, of each course of action.

Philosophers and preachers write volumes about the unknown and the unpredictable.

You and I are going to deal with what is knowable, predictable, provable, and true.

This book is a partnership between me and you. I am going to give you the tools to make sure that you understand your finances—what you own, what you want to own, and how it is going to provide the income you need to live the life you want. I am going to tell you what to read up on, and how to look at everything that comes your way, so you can find the gems that are right for you.

You are going to make yourself financially fit.

That is the goal of this book.

Finances are predictable. The steps you take now have a high degree of certainty in shaping what will happen later. Yes, some people will win the lottery, or inherit a windfall. But most of us won't. With finances, very little happens by chance. Take any financial situation, go back 50 years, and I can show you, at each point in time, how what you did caused the result that occurred. Similarly, give me any financial situation now, and I can reasonably project out 50 years what your money situation will be like.

It's not because I'm clairvoyant. It's just that I know what the rules are. I learned some by studying, (and some by not following the rules, and I paid the price). Your opportunity is to see if the points I make lead you to agree with my conclusions. If you do, you can apply my learning to your situation, without making the same mistakes. If not, you are welcome to make your own mistakes, or achieve your own successes, and I will take no responsibility in either case.

The financial world is logical, predictable, and foreseeable. Which means you can make plans, and cause desirable outcomes.

You just have to know the rules, and follow them.

But first, you have to commit to following RULE #1.

RULE #1: Understand your financial situation—know the answers to the following 8 questions. This is also known as the Financial Golden Rule: "Know Where the Gold Is!"

It is not good enough for your husband, wife, parent, or accountant to know your financial situation. You have to know. Mastering the subject matter of the lists in this book will get you to that goal. But before you start, you need to know the following:

1. What assets do you have?

2. Where are these assets?

3. What passwords do you need to access each? (It is not good enough to have them on a file in a computer. They need to be printed out, kept handy, and be coded so no one else can figure them out. More on how to do this later.)

4. Why do you own each asset? There has to be a reason it was purchased, and a reason you are holding onto it. (For instance: Asset—a 529 tax-free college fund. Reason purchased– to make sure there was money for college. Reason to keep–you are holding on to it because you will need money for college in 3 years, and it is performing well.)

5. What are your sources of income? Separate by earned (like salary) and passive (money that comes in when you work or not, like interest on a savings bond).

6. What are your expenses? How will they change in future years? You should be able to create a list of everything you spend in a year. You also need to be able to project how this will change in future years—add in money for unusual expenses that are anticipated. For retirement, add in the increased costs associated with aging poorly, such as some money for long term care. When making this list, focus on what

you spend money on, not how you pay for it. Credit cards are not a category of spending—food, clothing, personal care, entertainment are, even if you charge them. This is not as difficult as it sounds. Itemize everything you spend. Keep track of what you spend cash on.

7. What are your liabilities? What do you owe, to whom, how much, what are the payments, and what are the interest rates?

8. Know what is coming in down the road. Will you be inheriting any money in the future? Will you be inheriting any unfunded responsibilities? Is there anyone you will be responsible for taking care of in the future? As uncomfortable as it may be, you need to sit down with your parents periodically to review their financial situation. Vague promises that there will be something coming to you are not useful for planning.

Write down the answers to these questions. You will need this information to use this book.

The easiest way to stay on top of income and expenses is on a computer spreadsheet—see the example in Appendix A (use both pages). The difference between what you earn and what you spend is what you have to invest.

By the way, if you think you can ignore The Golden Rule, you might as well stop reading now. No one is going to be able to help you with your finances, no matter how much you pay them, unless you can draw a complete picture for yourself. And going out and buying financial products, like stocks, bonds, real estate, CD's, insurance, etc., will just create a financial mess that may or may not be beneficial to you.

In order to achieve **Financial Fitness**, you need to pay attention to the Financial Golden Rule.

So spend some time, review what you own and owe, and what you earn and spend, and put all the data together in one place, like the spreadsheets in Appendix A. Take the time to organize your passwords, and your list of what is where—it will be extremely helpful if someone other than you needs to get to your information. On a separate sheet, make notes on what you expect to happen in the future, as explained in item # 8 above.

Now you are ready for the 15 **Lists**. Please read the next section before you go any further. It will make the time you spend with this book much more beneficial.

USING THIS BOOK:

This book is separated into 15 sections, or **Lists**, that address key financial topics. The **Table of Contents**, on the preceding pages, is quite extensive. The objective was to provide a resource guide by areas of financial concern, for easy reference. You are welcome to go through the lists in the order they are printed. It may be helpful to do so in order to get an overall sense of what information is contained in each section, but it may be more beneficial to look at each topic as it becomes an area of interest for you.

LISTS #1 and **#2** are general in nature. Read them, even if they seem basic. Use the rest of the **Lists** to go into detail about particular financial issues that are of concern to you. These are the documents I give to my clients to read when they have questions about insurance and investments. As you will see, I have strong opinions. But they are based on facts. Some of the **Lists** cover a broad range of financial concerns, or address commonly held misconceptions. Others are more specific, such as the lists about long term care, disability insurance, and income security.

This book is meant to be neither a final authority, nor a complete compendium of useful information. My suggestion is that you use the material presented here to formulate questions, give you some background, and answer questions on financial matters that you may be less than fluent in. Then, use the Internet to research each area more completely— there is a tremendous wealth of information available from people who are not trying to sell you anything. Use the margins of the book to mark down websites that are helpful, and that you might like to go back to.

I'd also like to hear from you if you find errors, or explanations that are incomplete or not clear. If you think there are websites that I should visit to get more material, please let me know. The easiest way to contact me is though my website, www.InsuranceForEnhancedLiving.com.

You can also find the latest version of this book on the website, as well as more current information.

One blessing of 21st century technology is the ease at which you can research topics on your own. Check anything and everything you read on the Internet, especially before making a major financial decision. Evaluate the credentials of the writers of any information you use. Avoid letting others make decisions for you—read, and research, until you understand the facts, and make your own decisions. Planning for your financial future is complicated in scope, but understanding each of the pieces, and how they fit together, is something anyone can do, if you are willing to put in the time. The first thing I tell my clients is my job is to educate, to answer questions, to make suggestions. There is no one correct plan, or one correct financial product. There are various ways of getting to the same goals, with different instruments, and varying risks and rewards. There are never certain outcomes—much of sensible planning involves making assumptions about what you will earn, how healthy you will be, and when you will die. These are unknowns. But a financially sound portfolio of investments contains insurance that hedges your bets. It provides protection against uncertainty. The same should be true no matter who your financial advisor is. Only after you decide what appeals to you, and you both agree, should specific products be discussed.

Financial advising is a partnership. It should not be a sales pitch.

Use the **Lists** in this book as a starting point for your discussions.

Thank you.

DISCLAIMER: The opinions in this book are the author's, and the author's alone. The author is not writing on behalf of any insurance company or financial company, but solely as the CEO of the Berlin Consulting Group. Examples have been taken from published documents, or created by the author. Numbers are used for illustrative purposes only, to help describe what the author is explaining. Projections, rates, performance, etc.—anything dealing with numbers—are simply approximations and illustrations, and do not represent what has actually happened, or what will happen. They are used solely to explain concepts. All the numbers will always vary from what is shown when applied to a specific situation.

This material is not an offer to sell insurance or securities, which may only be done by a licensed professional who is properly registered, and who provides you with required disclosures. This material is merely the author's explanation of financial concepts. The examples of legal documents at the end of the book are just examples found on the Internet. Please do not use them to create your own legal documents for your use.

"I'm leaving you everything I own when I die, but until then, I need to live with you."

LIST 1: NINE SECRETS OF FINANCIAL PEACE OF MIND (HOW TO AVOID RUNNING OUT OF MONEY)

SECRET # 1. Start worrying (and saving) when you are young. Time is your friend.

If you put aside $100 a month starting on your 21st birthday, and invest it in a tax-free account that pays 5% compounded interest, on your 31st birthday you will have $15,792.

If you stop putting any more money in on your 31st birthday, on your 51st birthday you will have $43,180, which is enough to purchase outright the mid-life crisis car of your dreams.

In other words, $100 a month for 10 years (which is a total of $12,000), with interest, becomes $43,180 after 30 years. That is more than triple.

Let's say you are reading this, but you are now 51 or 61 years old. You're still young!!!! In 30 years, you'll be 81 or 91. You still have time to make this work for you. (If you are much older than 61 now, this section applies to your children or grandchildren. We'll discuss other strategies for you later.)

What you are doing is accessing the power of compounding. Invest a small amount today, and it will grow a little in one year. The next year it grows the same amount, but the earnings from the first year grow as well. In the third year, your original money still grows the same amount, but now the earnings from 2 years grow as well. Looking at it by decade, the first 10 years show slow growth. The next 10 years do a little better. Years 21-30 have a significantly higher growth curve, and in years 31-40, the growth is dramatic. If you have 5% annual growth, you'll end up with double your money in 15 years, or 7 times as much in 40 years. Even at a lower interest rate, like 3.5%, you still quadruple your money in 40 years.

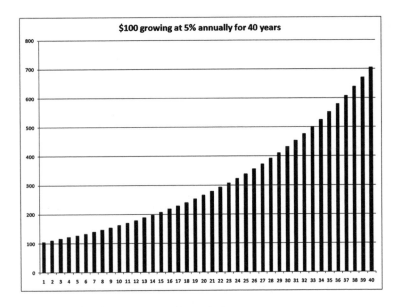

This raises 2 questions:

First, where are you going to find an extra $100 a month, which is $3.33 a day, roughly?

Here's a list of things that you can cut out of your daily routine to save $3.33 a day:

- A cup of trendy "coffee shop brand" coffee. (Sorry— my lawyers won't let me mention brand names, like Barstuck's. And this does not work if you live in

Chesnee, S.C., where the Bantam Diner charges 25 cents for a cup of coffee. However, the Bantam Diner does not fit the description "trendy," and you don't live in Chesnee, S.C.)

- The print edition of the New York Times ($2.00), and a doughnut (Krispy Kreme or Dunkin' Donuts, which you should not visit anyhow, unless you have the willpower to just get the coffee.)
- Any sweetened beverage, or two bottles of water, from a convenience store.
- One valet parking, every other day.
- One drink at a bar, every third day.
- Or you can start clipping coupons in the local Sunday paper. (If you start doing this, then you can continue to indulge in items 1 thru 5 above most days. You should be able to net $10-$15 off items you would already purchase via Sunday coupons.)
- Borrow, scrape, or scrounge cash wherever you can.

My point is, you are not talking a major lifestyle change to save $3.33 a day, which becomes $43,180, which is the price of a nice car, or the down payment on a vacation home. So you can either drink a cup of expensive coffee a day for the next 10 years, or you can drive a nice car or have a vacation home. It's your choice.

Now let's say you got into the habit of putting $100 a month aside, starting at age 21. After 10 years, you are 31 years old, and you have probably gotten used to not having the designer coffee. If you keep putting away the $3.33, by age 51, with compounding interest, you would have $84,648. The $100 a month for the additional 20 years would give you an extra $41,468. So now you've never had the designer coffee, but you own a motorboat, free and clear.

Let's say you don't read this until you are 31 years old, and you still want the motorboat. $100 a month won't do it. Now it will take a bit more than $202 a month for the next 20 years. In other words, if you indulge yourself at ages 21 to 30, you can still reach your goals, you'll just have to put more than twice as much aside later. That is harder to do.

The second question is, how are you going to consistently earn 5%, tax free, on your money for 30 years? It's not going to be in CD's, because you won't earn 5%, and what you do earn will be taxed, so it won't grow as fast year to year. It might be in stocks, bonds, or real estate, or other investments, but there is no guarantee, and it still gets taxed. There's only one way to do this that I know of, and we'll discuss that later.

SECRET # 2. Don't guess. Make a budget. Know what is coming in and going out.

It sounds trivial, but it's not. The biggest reason people get into financial trouble is that they spend more than they make. Period.

Your adult life is divided into two parts—the years you earn money by working, and the years you earn money from income on investments and retirement funds.

The goal of the first part (working) is to make sure there is enough money in the second part (passive income) to live the way you want to live. The added challenge is to wisely invest the surplus between what you earn and what you spend, during the first part of your life.

Spending more than you earn? That's your choice. But unless you are anticipating an inheritance or windfall, or expect to die young, be prepared for a lifestyle constrained by lack of money. Does this sound harsh? Too bad. It's true. You have two choices—learn it now, while you are young and can do something about it, or learn it later, when it is harder (but not impossible) to repair.

Don't like reading this? Fine, go see a Disney movie—one of the happy ones. Then re-read the above paragraphs. Pick the story you believe is true, and run with it. (Hint: Some Disney movies are called fairy tales for a reason.)

Budgeting: It is really simple. Go to any free website, and get a list of all the possible expense categories, or see Appendix A. Plug in what you spend monthly. Be realistic. If you don't know, start keeping track of each dollar. If you are spending more than you earn, figure out how to earn more, or where you can cut.

When I lived in New York on 24th Street, and worked on 49th, I would often walk to and from work on nice days. I passed about 6 Korean grocery shops. They always had a nice display of fruit outside, and it was easy to shop for a healthy dinner on the way home. The avenue in front of my apartment was one way, uptown. When I took the bus home on rainy days, I ended up on the downtown avenue, one block east. I discovered that produce there was 5 to 10 cents cheaper per item. A 3rd Avenue apple might cost 60 cents; on 2nd it was 50 or 55 cents. A few items a day could mean a 50 cents or $1.00 savings. I lived there for 4 years. When I left, one of the grocers on 3rd Avenue had bought up most of the buildings on the block. The guy on 2nd Avenue was still renting. Surprised?

Next, list all the money you earn. Sort it into two groups— the money you make by working (that is, the money that comes in as a result of your efforts), and the money you earn from investments (passive income that comes in whether you go to work or not). Then figure out how to increase each.

Your goal is maximize each type of income, and minimize expenses. The difference gets put into investments. It sounds simple, and it is, but most people don't do it. Some people think they can go to a financial planner, who will wave a magic wand, and come up with a plan for them. Which is what financial planners do. (That is, come up with a plan, not wave a wand.) But they are going to start with this same exercise. List your income. List your expenses. If you are not making more than you spend, they will kick you out of their office. Because no magic wand is going to create a stream of income that is not being spent, which is what you need to do in order to have a financial plan.

If you don't know how much you are spending, and how much you are making, you can't save, and you can't put money aside. You need to know the numbers, and you need to spend less than you make. Then you can develop a plan.

By the way, if you find that you are spending more than you are making, you really have just two choices. You can make more money, or spend less. You will find that it is easier to do the latter than the former. This brings me to SECRET #3:

SECRET # 3. Prioritize your spending.

There are two ways to have more money. One is to earn more. The other is to spend less.

And, as I said, earning more is the harder of the two.

Spending less means being conscious of how you spend money, so you can make changes. Fortunately, we live in a world of nearly limitless information. Anyone with computer access can easily and quickly find items to purchase at the lowest possible price. Offers and rewards abound, not just for things you don't need, but for things you would buy anyhow. It used to be that you would have to wait for a coupon or offer to come to you. On the Internet, you can seek these out.

Coupons, Groupon, decide what you want, find out how to get it for less.

You can get nearly perfect information before you spend money. Going out to eat?—chances are that you can find menus and coupons on-line, so that when you get to a restaurant, you'll know exactly what you'll be spending. It sure beats going to a trendy place and learning only after you've sat down that you'd rather spend less money at another place with food you prefer. Buying a car? You can almost price the one you want down to the penny, on-line. Clothing?—sales are advertised. Travel and leisure?—you've got to be kidding!—I can't find anyone who calls and makes reservations at published prices.

Don't have time to research bargains? Unlikely. There's plenty of down time—when you are in transit, waiting for an appointment, stuck on line, or fulfilling a social obligation by being present in body but not mind. There are plenty of times you have phone and wireless connections, so use them to plan your next savings. Discreetly. Effectively. Remember, even if you spend $3.33 less a day than you would have otherwise, that's $100 a month. Or a free motorboat—see above.

SECRET # 4. Avoid paying taxes. Make the government give you money. It's easy, and it is legal.

In 1913, the government first got the idea that it would be a great thing to charge people a tax on their income. Before that, taxes were imposed different ways—licenses, fees, taxes on certain goods, taxes on property, taxes on estates, etc. In some years, income tax rates soared—in the 1930's they went as high as 90% of earned income! Although the rate came way back down, it has gradually been creeping up again. And more taxes have been added—sales tax has been steadily growing, states and cities have added income taxes, and more and more products, like gasoline, tobacco, and alcohol, have additional excise taxes of their own. Parks used to be free, now they charge admission. It seems like everything is taxed. And that's because it is. Even if you are in the lowest income tax bracket, you end up paying a hefty amount in total taxes—often upwards of 50% of your income. When you die, you get whacked again, with estate taxes. And just in case you've figured out a way to reduce your taxes, the government makes you calculate them another way—the alternative minimum tax—to see if they can get you to pay more anyhow. It seems never ending, because it is. That's the price you pay for living in a great country like ours (and it is worth it). But the tax code, all ten thousand plus pages of it, contains hidden gems. There are many ways to reduce taxes—in effect, getting the government to give you money, instead of the other way around. It's legal, and it's easy. You just have to know how to play the game.

Essentially, there are three ways to handle taxes:
- you can pay as you go
- you can defer them until later
- you can make them go away

Everyone is familiar with pay as you go—that's what happens when you buy anything, or file annual tax returns.

Most people are familiar with deferring taxes—IRA's, 401k's, pension plans, annuities, etc. By investing or squirreling away money in a manner approved by Congress, you get to put off paying some taxes until later in life, when presumably, your income will be lower, and your taxes will be lower. But there are two caveats you need to be aware of:

1. If you manage your finances right, you can continue to pull in nice hefty earnings until late in life, so your tax rate might not drop at all, and
2. Who knows where taxes rates will go? If you look at the last 50 years, they've been creeping (or zooming) up. So the tax rate you have when your deferral period ends may be higher that it is now.

So that leaves us with the third option—investing money in a manner that is exempt from Federal income tax—money that grows tax-free, and comes to you or your heirs income tax free. You do this with life insurance products. They are the least understood of all financial products, and the ones people are most skeptical of. For good reason, as we'll see below. But before we do that, let me point out a side benefit. While insurance is making you money, it is also protecting your money. That because insurance has an added benefit—asset protection.

SECRET # 5. Protect your assets.

What's the point of making money if someone can just take it away from you?

It's not as dumb a question as it sounds. Until a little over a hundred years ago, the vast majority of all people on Earth were born poor, lived poor, and died poor. There were very few rich people, and they spent a lot of their wealth building castles with moats, hiring armies to attack potential enemies, and making sure that the people around them never accumulated enough money to take any time off from work, thus effectively preventing them from causing trouble. Almost everyone worked every day, and consumed all that they grew, traded, or crafted, with nothing left over. You got to stop working when you:

- Died, or
- Got too sick to work, in which case, unless someone gave you food, or you died, or
- Worked in vain, such as when disease or weather destroyed your crops or livestock, and you suddenly had no food, in which case, you got too sick to work, or starved, and you died.

The whole idea of retirement was a notion available to the select few—the powerful, and those who inherited wealth and who also had the strength to defend it. Well into the 1900's, and in many places until this day, people led, and still lead, a subsistence lifestyle, surviving from one harvest, hunt, or paycheck until the next.

But starting in the 1900's, a large middle class emerged—ordinary people who were able to earn more than it cost to live. They were able to put something away for the future, consume less than they made, and able to amass modest assets, or even wealth.

Suddenly, people had savings, and with that came the idea that these assets, if unprotected, could be taken away. That is when the modern concept of insurance as asset protection was born.

A brief history:

In the past, insurance existed in a limited fashion: *"The actual first known examples of the use of life insurance are associated with the Greeks around 1750 BC, when a sum of money was set aside for member of a household that was murdered during a robbery. It was during the times of the Roman Empire when the first mutual benefit associations, which provided their members with stated benefits and required regular contributions, were formed. During the Middle Ages, guilds developed more sophisticated forms of insurance, by covering a host of covered perils: death, illness, capture by pirates, shipwrecks, the burning of one's home and the loss of the tools associated with one's trade. In England, the first mutual groups of insurance were formed in connection with particular crafts or religions. They were called "Friendly Societies." In Muslim nations, where the Koran prohibits the payment of interest and gambling, Islamic insurers set up a tarajit, which is a form of life insurance. This is a collective pooling arrangement to protect heirs against unforeseen events that could financially hurt them." Barry Dyke, "The Pirates of Manhattan."*

In the Middle Ages, communities often pooled assets to redeem people captured and held for ransom. This practice created an ad hoc insurance fund. In some communities, piracy became so rampant that prominent religious leaders who were captured forbade their community to ransom them, in the hope of stopping the practice of piracy.

It may seem obvious, because insurance is so ubiquitous, but most insurance is a modern phenomenon:

- You have homeowners insurance, because you put a large down payment on your home, and if it blows away, floods, or catches fire, and you have to rebuild, you'll have a source of funds to do so. If you don't have insurance, you'll still owe the bank money, but you will have lost your down payment, and be homeless. (If you don't own, you have renters insurance, which protects the stuff in the home you rent.)
- You have health insurance, so that you can afford medical care if you get sick.
- You have car insurance, because the most likely way that you are going to get physically hurt in life is with

an automobile, and because the most likely way that you will hurt someone else is with an automobile, and if you don't have insurance, you may be held liable, and the person you hurt will be able to take away your assets.

- You have umbrella insurance, in case someone gets a judgment against you that is larger than the liability insurance you carry on your home or car.

Plus, some insurance is creditor protected, which means that you can put assets in an insurance policy, and know that if something bad happens—you hurt someone, you go bankrupt, you borrow money and cannot repay—there are some assets that will remain yours forever (notably life insurance and annuities). The more you have in protected assets, the more you get to keep and use, no matter what happens to you. Everything else—real estate, businesses, your gold coin collection, the money under your mattress, your bank accounts, and your prized first edition signed baseball card collection—can all be taken away.

SECRET # 6. Read the ads. Then, don't believe what you read. Acquire knowledge.

Here's the catch. People and businesses who are trying to get you to spend (your) money (at their place of business) have become very clever at figuring out what makes people want to spend money. And they know how to push just the right buttons to get you to part with money. Mainly, they promise you benefits that are worth more than you spend. Sometimes the benefits are real. Some toothpaste may get your teeth more sparkly than others, and some detergents may make your clothes cleaner. But whiter teeth are not likely to make you more popular, attractive, or successful in business. And slightly less than crisp colored clothing and bright white shirts won't be your ruination. Sure, while a bright smile may get you a tiny edge in being noticed, or sharp clothing may provoke a slightly warmer welcome, chances are that unless your grin is repulsive or your outfit slovenly, it is not going to make much of a difference in the long run. Same with a car. Or a purse. Or a brand of liquor. It doesn't matter. While the product may be "better" than a competitor's, the extra, intangible benefits are probably not going to materialize.

The same is true for other products and services. Not too long ago, there was an investment firm called E.F. Hutton. Their slogan was: "When E.F.Hutton talks, people listen." It was well known, and they spent millions associating this slogan with their brand. People still remember it. (Ask any 60 year old what happens when E.F. Hutton talks, and they'll tell you: "People listen.") The Hutton ads showed people in crowded, noisy rooms, and when one person said to another, "My broker is E.F Hutton, and he says..." the whole room fell silent. The implication is that the speaker was getting better investment advice than anyone else in the room because their advisor was E.F. Hutton. (It also implied that the speaker was a smarter person as well.) Never heard of E. F. Hutton? It was founded in 1904, and became one of the largest and most respected financial firms in the country. In 1980, one enterprising E. F. Hutton branch manager figured out that if he wrote a large check for more that the branch had available, and deposited it in another bank, it would take a few days to clear. (This was 1980, after all, and computers were slower and clunkier, and a lot of banks still used paper transactions.) He could cover this check a few days later with another one, and keep the process going forever. He advised headquarters of his scheme, which netted his branch an extra profit of $30,000 a month, and within three years, the firm was doing this with $250 million a day. When one bank caught on and notified the U.S. Attorney, Hutton at first denied the practice, then pleaded guilty to 2,000 charges of wire and mail fraud, and paid a penalty of over $10 million in 1985. In 1987, an internal probe revealed that one branch was laundering money for the Mafia, and the government prepared to indict the firm. As luck would have it (or not), the next week, in October, 1987, the market crashed, and Hutton lost $76 million, and the investigation got sidetracked. When Hutton merged with another firm in early 1988, it was revealed that it had been facing massive cash shortages since 1985, and had been secretly up for sale since 1986. Several mergers later, the name is gone, and conversations don't stop (if they ever did), when people mention E.F. Hutton. While they were around, they did no better or worse for clients than other similar firms. If you had your investments with them, you may have felt that you were better off. You weren't.

So the lesson is: read the ads. They have valuable information. But be skeptical. If a benefit seems unrealistic, it probably is. If claims can't be substantiated, they're probably illusory. With all the access you have to the Internet to easily check facts, shame on you if you fall for hype.

It costs money to advertise. The only money these firms earn comes from the money you give them to manage. The more advertising you see, the higher their expenses are. Which means that your gains are lower. (See **LIST #5: Nine Qualities to Look for in a Financial Advisor**.)

Let me clue you in on some inside information about Secret #6. You are going to read and hear two types of advisory messages: advertising and expert opinions. Advertising is paid for by people who have a vested interest in you believing what they have to say. The information stated may or may not be true. Some industries, like insurance, are highly regulated, so there actually is a very good chance that advertising information is accurate. But it is still trying to get you to buy something. The products they are pushing might be good products. But they might not be good for you, or good for you at this point in time, or the best for you. They just might be great for someone else who sees or hears that same ad. But you are going to have to make that determination yourself, based on your knowledge, and based on advice you sift through.

The appropriateness of expert opinions for you has similar problems. The experts may be smart, and their recommendations good for some people, but unless they know who you are, and what your needs are, they have no way of broadcasting a message that is accurate for all their listeners. And if you are dealing one on one with an expert, they are either being paid an hourly fee to advise you, or a commission, which means they don't get paid if you don't buy. In the first case, you don't know how much the expert knows, and you don't know if he knows what is right for you, and in the second case, well, do you think that a commission salesperson is unbiased? When I sell insurance, I work on a commission basis. And I have to force myself to try to think independently, without biases that I naturally pick up by reading professional literature. I'm not sure all my contemporaries fight the same fight—it is too easy to just push the product that is easiest to sell, pays the most, or that you are most familiar with.

Also, when you read so-called independent write-ups or hear investigative reports, who do you think is doing the writing or reporting? An expert? No, it is done by writers and reporters. Who call people who they think might be experts (like me) to ask questions and get input for their stories. (I know—I get calls all the time.) They are not experts themselves on the issues—they are just expert writers and reporters. So the story that gets produced is not always accurate or impartial. I know—I read them daily, and shake my head at the advice given. I have a burgeoning file of stories I've collected from respected financial publications, offering what is just plain old bad and wrong advice.

SECRET # 7. Find advisors who are smarter than you.

Don't take what they say at face value—ask questions. Make them prove that they understand the products they sell, and why those products are right for you. Avoid canned sales pitches—make them explain what they are proposing in their own words. (See **LIST #5: Nine Qualities to Look for in a Financial Advisor.**)

Take financial advice from people you respect. But don't take it at face value. Demand proof of claims they make. If you don't understand something, make them explain it to you until you do. It has to make sense for it to be real. Don't be fooled by numbers and charts—understand the claims being made. If claims are too good to be true, they probably aren't true. If they are wildly different from claims competitors are making, they are probably not accurate. There are only two possibilities with financial products if they promise a lot more than anyone else: either they are losing money, or lying. If they are losing money, they won't be around for very long, so you'll never get the returns promised. And if they're lying, well... You read the newspapers, don't you? Insurance is a highly regulated industry. For a reason. There are lots of disclosures. Read them.

SECRET # 8. Wear x-ray goggles.

Not literally. But pretend you are. Why are you being shown something? What's behind the recommendation? What's the reason your advisor feels this product is most appropriate for you? Why is one product being recommended over another?

There are a huge range of financial products available. One person can only be familiar with a portion of them. It is the natural inclination of a salesperson to find several products that they like, become familiar with them, and recommend them to any clients. They usually do this with the best of intentions—they've done the research, and they've found something that appeals to them, so they use it.

You bring to the discussion an intimate knowledge of your needs, preferences, and concerns—something that no one else knows. There may be products out there that your advisor is not familiar with that better address your needs. You may need to find them yourself, or direct your advisor to look for them. The value of wearing x-ray goggles is that you can use them to tell if a product is right for you.

When in doubt, ask.

If you don't get answers that make sense, get them, or leave.

Are the benefits being offered real, or illusory? Feeling good is great, but understanding why you are feeling good is better. It's no shame to say "I don't understand this." If it can't be explained to you, you either have the wrong product, or the wrong teacher. The financial crisis of 2008/2009 was caused in large part by people (sophisticated, intelligent people) trading financial instruments they did not understand.

Don't rely on the government to protect you. Yes, they will pass laws to outlaw people doing bad things to you, but only after a pattern emerges, and there are enough victims. Yes, they will prosecute bad people, but only after the damage is done. Bad people will always figure their way around protective barriers—if you don't go opened-eyed into every financial presentation, you run the risk of being *the* case that causes the government to react—after you have been hurt, and when it will help others in the future, but not you.

But even good, well intentioned advisors may not come up with the best products for you, unless you can help them evaluate the appropriateness of what they recommend for your situation.

SECRET # 9. Play offense and defense at the same time.

I prefer not to use sports analogies, because they only work for some people. But this one is pretty basic. Think of your money and assets as being on two squads of your team. The offensive money is working hard, trying to grow, and pursuing opportunities, taking risks, trying to get ahead. But sometimes your defensive squad will be on the field, protecting what you've gained. Sometimes the game will not be going your way. It is important to have money and assets in reserve, responding to different stimuli in the marketplace, so that when one sector is not doing well, you don't have to go into those funds at the wrong time. For example, real estate is a proven venue for making money. The key is buying low, producing income, and selling high. But you have little control over the marketplace. There will be times when rents don't cover expenses. There will be times when you'll need quick access to cash. If too much money is tied up in real estate (an offensive position), and you need cash, you may be forced to sell at the wrong time. By having a portion of your assets invested in defensive, safe, cash-rich, judgment-proof investments, which may grow more modestly than your offensive assets, you provide a safe balance to your portfolio, and a place to get cash when selling the real estate isn't ideal. Stocks are also offensive positions—but a downturn can last a while, and make them illiquid. The goal is to never be caught where you are forced to dip into assets that are not doing well.

If you are just starting your earning career, it is easy to play offense and defense at the same time. If you are close to retirement, it is a little harder, but a proper balance of investments can insure that you have the income you need while preserving capital. It depends on how well you allocate your portfolio.

What do I mean by defense? Cash, annuities, life insurance, short-term bonds—anything with a near zero chance of loss of principal.

What is offense? Anything with risk but also potential for big gains.

Now, let's go back to the $43,180 and $84,648 worth of designer coffee! (See SECRET #1 above.)

We started by talking about $1,200 a year for ten years. If you started on your 21st birthday, and used $1,200 a year for ten years to buy a "whole life" life insurance policy, and you were in excellent health, using standard illustrations, you would have about $75,000 in cash available to you, tax-free, to use as you wish, on your 51st birthday, PLUS, you would have an insurance policy worth over a quarter of a million dollars. If you started at 51 or 61, it would take the same 30 years— you'd just be older when you reaped the rewards, and the insurance policy would be worth less.

Here's how this works:

First, let's start out with an understanding of life insurance. Most people confuse life insurance with death insurance. That's because they think of "term life" insurance when someone mentions life insurance, and for good reason—term life insurance is what most people buy because (surprise), that is what most insurance companies want you to buy, because it is a product that they make tons of money on, and they rarely ever pay out the face value. Here's why:

Term life insurance is a contract between you and an insurance company, where you agree to pay them a certain amount every year (the "premium") and they agree to pay you (actually, your heirs) a huge sum, many times the amount of the premium, if you die within a certain period of time, say 20 years. Generally, the premium is the same every year, although some policies start with extremely low premiums, which increase each year. As long as you pay the premium each year, your heirs get the benefit promised if you die. Once you stop, the deal is off. All the money you paid is gone. There is no residual value. The policy has no value. It's over. And if you happen to live one day longer than the term you contracted for, same thing—no policy, no coverage, no benefits, no value. So if you had paid in $1,000 a year, every year, for 20 years, with a 20 year term policy, and you died twenty years and a day later, it's as if the insurance company never had an agreement with you. They keep all the premiums, and your heirs get nothing. I've read somewhere that over 98% of terms policies never pay out— either people stop paying the premiums, or they die after the policy period is over. Maybe a more accurate number is 90%, or even 80%. It doesn't matter. The vast majority of these policies never pay out. Young people simply don't die within 20 years of taking out term insurance. And if you go to renew the insurance when it expires—surprise! The rates have jumped astronomically. And your health may have deteriorated to the point at which you are charged even more just to get coverage, or you may be declined coverage completely.

"Permanent" polices differ in that they either build some sort of cash value in addition to a death benefit, or they have a death benefit that is guaranteed, no matter how long you live. Some are designed so that you only pay premiums until a certain age, and others you pay until age 100. In some cases, if you build sufficient cash value, or if the policy pays dividends, you can stop paying premiums early, and even withdraw some of the cash value as a loan to be paid off from the death benefit when you die.

About 50 years ago, an insurance company came up with the slogan: "Buy term and invest the difference." It was catchy, and it got to the point. You could get insurance coverage very inexpensively, and then invest what you had saved by not having bought a whole life policy. But what really happened was that people saved on the premium, but spent the rest, instead of saving it. And what they did not tell you is that if you had put it all with the insurance company, they could have invested the money better and more safely than you could, and that it would have grown tax free.

With a permanent policy, unlike term insurance, you will always get a return on your money, either before death, or when you die. **And because Congress wants to encourage this sort of insurance, the growth of your money inside the policy is income tax free, and the benefit paid to your heirs is income tax free (but still subject to estate tax), and money you borrow out of the policy is income tax free, and non-reportable.** As long as you do not outright cancel the policy, or let it lapse, you never have to pay income taxes on it. And because your money can grow year after year, without taxes, it can grow faster than money in a taxable account. (This tax-free benefit only works if you play by the rules—you have to be careful when you set up these policies, and when you take money out, to make sure that you do not do anything that would make the proceeds taxable.)

There are also other insurance products, such as annuities, that let income grow tax-deferred.

These let you earn money now, and pay tax on it later.

Overall, the point I am trying to make is that there are several ways to make your money work harder for you—it can grow at the 5% you need to buy that home or boat, plus it can provide a death benefit. And having a guaranteed death benefit means you can spend assets now, because they will be replenished when you die. So not only can you buy the car or boat with your $3.33, you can still leave your heirs a tidy sum.

I'm an advocate for whole life insurance. I make a lot of money selling it. But I've also been treated well by the policies I own. It is not a sexy investment—nobody is going to get excited about the returns. But it is a sensible investment. The returns are steady, and the payout is secure, and large. I believe that it should be a core component of everyone's financial fitness regime. You will see, at various points in this book, how whole life insurance works, and what it can do for you.

"How can I be out of money? I still have checks left!"

LIST 2: SEVEN RULES
FOR MANAGING YOUR FINANCES

RULE #1: Know what your assets are.

Understand key financial terms, and how they apply to you. At the very minimum, learn these terms, especially if you or your spouse own any of these:

- **Mutual fund**—a pool of money gathered from many people, and invested in specific assets, or groups of assets. You pay a management fee to have someone handle this for you, which can be paid up front when you buy, or when you sell, or a combination of the two. They can go up or down in value. You can trade these through a broker. They are very liquid.
- **Stocks**—ownership of shares in a corporation. For public companies, these are traded on stock exchanges, and are very liquid. For private companies, they may be bought and sold by individuals, and can be very hard to sell at times.
- **CD's**—a bank issued product that pays a fixed rate of interest, over a fixed period of time. Principal is guaranteed by the bank, and insured by the government. You may pay a penalty for cashing them in early.
- **Money Market**—interest bearing accounts, insured by the government. No obligation on your part to keep

the money in the account for any specific period of
time. No penalties to redeem.

- **Bonds**—loans to corporations or government, paying
a fixed interest rate, maturing on a fixed date. They
can vary in value, and it is possible for the borrowing
entity to default, leaving you with a worthless
investment. They go up or down in value, and are
easily sold.
- **Cash value life insurance**, also called permanent life
insurance and whole life insurance. This has a death
benefit, and an investment portion that provides
cash that can be withdrawn or borrowed. If issued by
a mutual company, you will earn dividends. You can
cash out at any time, but most people access the cash
value by borrowing from the policy, and paying back
the loan from the proceeds when they die. This has
beneficial tax implications.
- **Term life insurance**—pays a death benefit if you die
within the term of the policy, usually ten or twenty
years. No benefit if you die later. No cash value.
- **Variable annuity**—offered through insurance
companies. You pay premiums once or periodically,
they are invested in subaccounts or investment
portfolios, and the value of your contract fluctuates,
or varies, over time, according to how well the
investments perform. You generally have an option
on which funds to invest in. Variable annuities can
have a lot of bells and whistles, such as guaranteed
minimum payouts (irrespective of performance), and
guaranteed death benefits. However, there are a lot
of variations on these features, and they all carry a
cost, which is taken out of the contract value. You can
always get your principal back, but in the first few years

(the number of years varies with the product), there is a withdrawal penalty.

- **Fixed annuity**—no guesswork involved. You know upfront what your earnings will be, and how they will be paid out. However, you can get a hybrid—a fixed index annuity, which has a guaranteed minimum benefit, with upside potential. Fixed annuities also have withdrawal penalties, but they can be designed to start producing regular income as early as one month after you make the initial premium.

But that's just an overview. There are more. If you own anything that is not listed above, learn about it. Each product has unique features, and specialized terms used to describe these features. Fortunately, each financial instrument is required to disclose these factors, although rarely in easily understood language. That's where the Internet is helpful— there are a lot of sites that explain these terms, and you'll always find product specific information, posted by either the seller, or someone who has bought the product and found out that it was not what they thought it was.

You need to understand the nature of every asset you own. In particular, you need to know:

- What did you pay for it?
- What is it worth now?
- How does it increase or decrease in value, and under what conditions?
- What amount of income does it provide you on a regular basis?
- What will it cost you to convert it to cash? (what are the tax consequences, how long will it take, what will you end up with, etc.?)
- How might it change in value in the future?

RULE #2: Know how to access your assets.

Keep a secure and easily accessible list of passwords, combinations, and locations of keys. Some of your financial assets may have papers associated with them—sometimes crucial papers, like original notes or certificates, and sometimes just convenient papers, like life insurance policies, which can always be replaced. Some of what you own may be jointly owned, in which case you need to also know who else has to be with you to get access to these assets. Much of what you own is registered online, or stored in something that is locked—a safe, or a bank safe deposit box. You need to keep a physical list—not just a list in your computer—that says what you have, and where it is. It needs to have your passwords as well, and your passwords need to be encrypted, with a code that is obvious to people who you want to have access to your assets, and incomprehensible to everyone else. For instance, pick a combination of letters and numbers that are random, and known only to you, and embed them in every password. Make sure two other people know this code—people you trust. For instance, let's say you pick "L7g5H." That becomes part of every password you use, but on your printed password list, if you have a password such as "RachelL7g5H," just write is as "Rachel*". Then make sure two people, like your spouse and your lawyer, have a document that says "*=L7g5H" in case something happens to you, or you forget the secret, or develop amnesia.

RULE #3: Know what your assets are worth.

Know their cost and current value.

You need to know cost for one reason, and one reason only—do you have a loss that will reduce your taxes, or a gain that will increase them?

You need to know current value for one reason, and one reason only—what is a realistic projection of future value?

Note that nowhere in these figures is the calculation of what percent loss or gain you have, or the idea of holding onto a losing asset until it recovers. The past is important only insofar as tax gains or tax losses are concerned. There is no room for sentimental attachment or wishful thinking. A decision to hold an asset is no different than a decision to go out and buy it today (except for tax concerns). If you would not buy the asset today, chances are that you should not be holding it—your money is better invested in an asset that will perform well.

RULE #4: Know how to measure the performance of your assets.

Track them year to year. Know their growth potential. Get rid of the losers—don't be sentimental. See RULE #3 above.

RULE #5: Know what your long-term goals are.

Know what cash value you need to have at any point in your life, and make sure your assets can be converted to cash without a loss, or without giving up financial opportunities, when you need the cash. The key point of any financial portfolio is not its value, but your ability to convert parts to cash as you need it without hurting its value, and without hurting its ability to replenish its value. This is sometimes referred to as the "buckets" theory—thinking of your assets as being kept into discreet buckets, which perform differently under the same market conditions. This assures you that some of your portfolio will always be growing, and that some will always be accessible without hurting you. See LIST #8 and LIST #9 for a full explanation of the "buckets" theory and how it works.

Use the LISTS in this book to start your learning about various aspects of managing your finances so you can reach your goals. Go beyond this book to become intimately familiar with the financial products you own, and how they fit in to your long term plan.

RULE #6: Know who to talk to.

Have many advisors; know the strengths and weaknesses of each.

Know your personality, and what motivates you. If you are a salesperson type, chances are that you'll fall for other people's sales pitches—salespeople believe their own stories— so you need to avoid commission based sales people, and any other sales person as well. If you are analytical and detached, salespeople are fine to deal with—you'll know how to push past the sales hype to ascertain the true appropriateness of whatever is being invested.

The best thing about living in the Internet age is that you can check out anything online. Someone is always out there offering advice, information, and instruction, and someone else is always there with a rebuttal. It's amazing how much is out there, and it's amazing how much people don't use the resources. Want a better explanation of anything I've discussed in this book? Google it! A client of mine called attention to a full-page ad in the local paper, which costs about $10,000 to run, touting the services of a particular investment advisor, and guaranteeing 9.5% returns. So I Googled the name, and the first thing that pops up is a story on how he was disbarred in Nevada and Pennsylvania. Then came stories about lawsuits against him. Then came his website, with glowing praise, and nary a word about the administrative actions pending against him in 20 states, which I had just learned from reading the headlines of the links that popped up—without ever opening a page! Was this man stupid – paying $10,000 for an ad when he had such a blemished record? Didn't he know that people would check on him, and he would never get a dollar's worth of business from his investment in advertising? I got my answer the following month, when he ran the ad again. He figured, correctly, that enough people would not even do basic, minimal research, and he made so much money the first time he ran the ad, he felt it was worthwhile to do it again. Then I found an article published by a law firm that claims that more than 40,000 retirees and seniors attend his seminars every year. It quotes a Bloomberg article (9/11/2007—Susan Antilla): "He is a former lawyer with a checkered past.... Resigned from the Florida Bar in 1997 after receiving two consecutive 6-month suspensions on the heels of four previous public disciplines…"

RULE #7: Plan your income stream.

Know what is coming in, and when, and make sure it exceeds what is going out. Until you retire. Then you can spend more than is coming in, if:

- You have a guaranteed stream of income that is sufficient to meet your needs for the rest of your life. See **LIST 9: Understanding Annuities (Income Security in Retirement)**

- You have assets that will replace whatever you are spending now. See **LIST 6: Eight Insurance Mistakes to Avoid**
- You've taken care of the added expenses of aging poorly. See **LIST 11: Three Facts You Need to Know About the Cost of Aging (Long Term Care)**

If not, you still have to spend less than you make, even in retirement.

"I figured I paid for the kid's college, so I should be able to get a scholarship for retirement?"

LIST 3: THREE FINANCIAL MYTHS, AND WHAT THE TRUTH IS

MYTH #1: Stocks.

Fortunes have been made and lost in the stock market. Markets have peaked and fallen. Since trading stocks underneath the big oak tree in colonial times, the financial system has revolved around the stock exchanges.

Those days are over. The markets are primarily electronic now, and trading is done by high speed computers using elaborate algorithms. The individual investor is a winner or loser not by his or her own actions or calculation, but as a consequence of what positions he or she owns when the big players make their moves.

Forget history. The stock markets are a new paradigm, connected to what they were in the past by name only. No one knows how they will work in the future, least of all the major players.

Play at your own risk, hedge your bets. The stock markets are still where financial news is made, as well as fortunes. But it is not a place for amateurs. Use professionals.

MYTH #2: Housing.

It used to be that owning a home was a good investment, not because it cost less than renting, but because, over time, values were certain to rise.

This is no longer the case. In markets where there is a glut of inventory, prices may still be sinking. In nearly any market, the cost of owning is significantly greater than the cost of renting. More and more people are going to come to the conclusion that owning a home does not make financial sense. Too many people will let the emotional need to own a home override financial prudence.

If you want to own a home, do it knowing that it is a luxury that you choose to spend money on for your own amusement. It is not a decision governed by a profit motive.

That being said, I have to acknowledge that it depends on timing, specific markets, and your time frame. I personally have done very well owning real estate. I've bought and sold commercial and residential properties.

In many cases, I was able to buy at low points in the market. Real estate is cyclical, and I was able to time my purchases right. That is not always possible.

I had staying power. I never had to sell prematurely. My rental properties stayed rented. I had minimal tenant problems. You have little control over this. Often, I was able to buy right because others had to sell, due to market and/or rentability issues. I benefited, they lost.

I was able to add value to some of the properties I owned. That increased their selling prices. But those are rental properties. And sometimes I was just lucky.

My successes do not change my opinion of real estate. If you want to go into it as a business, if you know what you are doing, if you can withstand extended adverse situations— fine. Invest in real estate. But often as not, investing in a home, and living in it, will not be the best way to build a retirement portfolio. In America, we have a bias towards home ownership. In Europe, more people rent. But you can't look backwards in real estate, and project forward. The appreciation we saw after WWII until the 1980's may not happen again. People are more mobile, and our parents' generation's tendency to buy a home and stay in it for life will not be our experience, no more than will we take a job in our 20's and retire from that same job in our 60's.

Newspapers are full of articles telling us when it is and is not a good time to buy. Often, different newspapers say opposite things—buy or rent—at the same time. Sometimes, the same newspaper says both. But you have to remember, newspapers make a lot of money on real estate ads—both "for sale" and "for rent" ads. And real estate agents, part of a huge industry (note: I have a real estate broker license), only make money when you buy, sell, or rent. If we all stayed put for our entire lives, there would be no real estate agent industry. So exhortations about buying or renting now may be motivated not by what is good for you, but by what produces income for the exhorter.

Owning your own home is not a slam dunk. It does not have to go up in value. You can end up putting a lot of money in, and not getting a good return. It can be less expensive, in total, to rent. And if there is any chance that you will be forced to move when you do not want to sell, you may be stuck owning a rental property (which used to be your home) in a city you don't live in any more.

Like the stock market, the game is different now, and so are the rules. Be careful.

MYTH #3: College.

The question is not whether or not you should save for college. The question is: what is the opportunity cost of doing so?

In other words, if you save for college, what are you diverting money from?

Most people fail to consider the obvious—if you save for college, what are you not saving for? And if you spend money on college, what do you not have money left for? And, if you don't have money saved for college, how will you pay for college? But if you don't have money saved for retirement, how will you pay for retirement?

College is going to last four years, there are scholarships and loans available, and if you cannot afford one particular college, you can always find another that you can afford. On the other hand, retirement is going to come whether you save for it or not, it will last for decades, and there are no scholarships or loans available. The quality of your life in retirement is going to be commensurate with the income you've provided for. If you don't plan your retirement, Medicaid and social security will, and it may not be the retirement you envision. Also, consider the following: if you follow the rules, and put aside money for college, and don't have enough, you'll apply for financial aid. First, they'll take the money you've saved, be it in a 529 plan or something else, and then they'll consider your needs, and loan or give you the rest. But if you don't save specifically for college, and instead put the same money in retirement vehicles, when it comes time for college, if you don't have enough money, they'll make you come up with less, and loan or give you the rest. In short, unless you can save for both college and retirement adequately, look out for your retirement needs first, then save for college. Don't believe the hype. Sure, colleges want you to pay for your children's education, because that way it will cost them less. But ask the financial aid office—"If I pay for college in full, will you loan or give me money for retirement?" If they won't, make sure you put your retirement needs first.

College costs way more than it did for your parents. And retirement for you will be longer, and more expensive. Approach college and retirement with open eyes—it's a different game than it was 30 years ago, so you need to plan accordingly.

"That's right, you're my new financial advisor. It says right here in the newspaper: Pick someone who listens to you attentively."

LIST 4: NINE QUALITIES TO LOOK FOR IN A FINANCIAL ADVISOR

QUALITY #1: The ability to listen.

Your situation is unique. Describe it to your advisor. Tell him or her what your needs are. Know your goals. Can he or she repeat it back to you, without notes? If not, find a different advisor—this one isn't listening.

QUALITY #2: The ability to communicate clearly.

Repeat back your understanding of what you are being told. Make your advisor explain the abbreviations to you. Make sure you understand what they stand for, and how concepts apply to you. Too good to be true usually is—remember, highly sophisticated people fell for Ponzi schemes and the collateralized debt obligations (CDO's) that sunk Lehman Brothers and major banks. Most people who sold CDO's did not understand them. Read any of the books about the collapse of 2008, most notably Barry Dyke's "The Pirates of Manhattan" to see just how frighteningly ignorant the greedy and overpaid salespeople/con artists who ran major funds and banks were. They did not know about what they were buying and selling. Don't stop there—go back and read about the tulip bulb craze of the

1620's in Holland. Put the two together, and you'll see that in 400 years, nothing has changed: clever people who are willing to take advantage of others can always find someone gullible.

QUALITY #3: The ability to see you as an individual.

Your financial situation and your goals are unique to you. How customized is the proposed solution that is presented to you. How well does each piece address your needs?

QUALITY #4: Competency, and intelligence.

Check references. Who does the person work with? What is his or her reputation? What are his or her strengths? What do all the letters after his or her name mean? Google each one—if he or she is boasting credentials that require just membership in an organization, and no experience or qualifying education, be suspicious. (Mary L. Shapiro, the CEO of FINRA—a government group responsible for regulating the financial industry—said on 9/10/2007 about a pending regulatory action: "The first sweep is aimed at the use of inflated or meaningless titles by advisers who are seeking to lure seniors into thinking they are experts in retirement planning. The use of so-called professional designations is becoming an increasingly common device used to open an account. The unfortunate truth is that seniors can be susceptible to these tactics. Our research shows that some seniors are more likely to listen to pitches from people with such designations.... The unfortunate fact is that some designations can be obtained by simply paying membership dues to an organization with an impressive sounding name.

Too many times these designations mean absolutely nothing. Seniors put their trust in these individuals and are led down a path of financial ruin."

QUALITY #5: Connectivity.

Who does your advisor go to for advice? No advisor can know everything—the key is knowing where to go to learn what is right for you. Who are his or her advisors?

If your advisor cannot call on a wide range of experts to fashion a solution for you, it means he or she is regularly selling a small set of products that he or she knows well, and is not open to spending time to learn what is best for you. Can he or she run through a "what if" scenario with you? Provide reasonable projections of your financial trajectory? Summarize recommendations clearly? Or is it a hodge-podge?

QUALITY #6: Concern.

This is my biggest area of annoyance. Too many advisors are sales motivated—find the client, present a product, make the sale, collect the commission, move on. You need to flip it around. It's your money, and your future. The commission payout of most products is huge. Your advisor has to be looking at your situation from your perspective. He or she is being well compensated. There is only one chance to get it right. You'll never have a chance to go back thirty years and begin your earning experience over again. If an advisor implies that you are taking up too much time, or asking too many questions, or looking for too many quotes, then it's not a right fit for either of you. Leave.

QUALITY #7: Compatibility.

Unless you share similar values, it's hard for your advisor to get on your wavelength. I'm not talking about sharing hobbies, or even community involvement. What I am speaking about is those values that lead to hobbies and community involvement. Priorities, ethics, the role each of you plays in the community. You are talking about plans that will shape your life, and your children's lives. Don't you want to do this with someone who has the same values as you?

QUALITY #8: Confidentiality.

Are you being told things about other clients that you would not want other people to know about you? If so, leave. When you go to your advisor's office, are other client files readily visible? When you view files on your advisor's computer, do you end up glimpsing information about other clients? Are your advisor's files labeled with client names, or is each client assigned a discrete number? (I limit the use of names on physical and computer files so that there is maximum privacy. And I don't tell clients or potential clients the names of other clients, unless I have specific permission to do so.)

QUALITY #9: Follow through.

Does your advisor follow through when promised, in a reasonable timeframe? Don't expect immediate answers— developing recommendations can take time, and you are one of several clients. But your advisor needs to be able to acknowledge your inquiries, respect your time horizons, and follow through on delivering information when promised. If he or she doesn't, leave. That person is either too busy for you, or you are not important enough for him or her.

Either way, it's a bad fit for you.

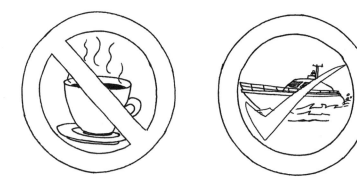

Your choice—a cup of designer coffee a day for 10 years, or owning a motorboat.

LIST 5: THE BENEFITS OF STARTING TO SAVE (AT ANY AGE)

Example 1:

About seven years ago, when I first started looking at the growth in the value of my permanent policies, someone suggested that I take out policies on the children's' lives. At first, I scoffed. I didn't have spare money, and they didn't have anyone to leave an estate to. But I saw the growth that had occurred in my policies, so I did it anyway. I'm glad I did. Here's why:

Buying insurance for children, teenagers, or young adults is inexpensive. The same premium dollars buy them a lot more insurance than it will buy an adult. For instance, I was able to buy some of the children the same amount of insurance that I had bought myself at age 39 for half the price. (I selected a flat rate that I was willing to pay, and bought the maximum coverage for that price. Naturally, I paid less for the girls than the boys, and less for the younger ones than the older ones.) And because I bought from a solid company, with a good history, I built cash value in excess of the projected returns. (Caveat: under age 18, the children are rated as juvenile, which is a blended rate—they don't do physical exams and individual underwriting. Once they turned 18, I had them re-rated. Because they are healthy, the insurance portion of the premium decreased, and the amount applied to investments increased, thus bumping cash value further.)

The benefits:

After six years, the cash value is growing at an amount greater than the premium. This means that I can borrow cash from the policy, and use it to pay the premium. In other words, the cash value is now growing with no further cash outlay on my part. This actually would have been possible earlier, but I waited until now.

When I purchased the policies, I kept my wife and myself as the owners, for two reasons: One, some of the children were still minors. Two, by retaining ownership, we retained control, which is a good idea while the children are still young adults. Plus, we owned the cash value, so if, unfortunately, anything happened to us and we needed the money, we would be able to access it. We can always gift it over to the children at a later date. (Depending on the cash value, there could be tax issues that would cause us to have to gift the policies over time, or in a certain fashion, but the benefits of retaining control seem to outweigh the hassles in doing a later gifting.)

Paying for the policies for 5 years can be a challenge. But you have to look at what resources are available. Grandparents? Savings bonds that they got at birth and matured after 10 or 15 years? Their piggybank/birthday gift accounts that are earning .0000005% at the bank?

Example 2:

Now that I've built cash value, I took the next step. I took out additional policies, with a twist. These newer policies, which are in addition to the existing policies, and not a replacement, build cash value at a lower rate, and therefore provide more coverage for the same premium dollars, but they have an important feature that I hope the children will never use. These policies allow the withdrawal of a portion of the death benefit in case the insured needs long-term care. I cringe to think of it—it is too horrible to image. But conceivably, the need could arise, before any of the children had a disability policy. (They will not have meaningful disability coverage until they earn meaningful incomes, which is a while off.) And the financial effect of paying for long-term care for the children would be devastating without insurance. The beauty of this policy is that it is a regular, permanent policy, so it grows in value, and has benefits that will pass on to my children in the prime of their lives, or for my yet-to-be-born grandchildren (from my yet-to-be-married children), when my children are old. In other words, unlike long term care insurance, which you may never, if you are lucky, have to draw on, these policies will have cash value while the children are healthy, and substantial benefits when they eventually die, in 80 or 100 years.

The net result is that for a (small) original investment over half a dozen years, I've given my children a tremendous head start on financial security, added to my safety net, and helped two or more generations that will follow me.

Example 3:

You can also use the strategy of insuring children to prolong the benefits of an annuity designed to produce income. By using a joint annuity, where one annuitant is significantly young than the other, you get income now (at a lower rate), but you or your heirs will get it for a generation or two longer.

Example 4:

Start saving small amounts regularly. It adds up. See SECRET #1 in **LIST 1: Nine Secrets of Financial Peace of Mind.**

"There's no need to actually read the policy—it's all just as you've seen on TV!"

LIST 6: EIGHT INSURANCE MISTAKES TO AVOID

The 8 most common insurance mistakes people make:

MISTAKE #1: People confuse life insurance with death insurance.

MISTAKE #2: Death insurance is expensive (but looks cheap) and is usually a waste of money.

MISTAKE #3: Most people insure themselves against the losses that are least likely to occur, and don't insure against the most likely losses.

MISTAKE #4: Most people don't understand the insurance they buy.

MISTAKE #5: Nobody reads the sales literature and the policy.

MISTAKE #6: People pay premiums monthly.

MISTAKE #7: Most people set up their retirement plans so that they'll run out of money before they die.

MISTAKE #8: People complain about taxes, but ignore the opportunities to avoid taxes, legally.

MISTAKE #1: People confuse life insurance with death insurance.

Death insurance pays you a benefit when you are dead. This is also known as term insurance. Permanent insurance is life insurance—it provides financial benefits while you are alive. It lets you spend your money. When you die, the death benefit replaces the money you've spent.

Term insurance is insurance that pays a death benefit in the event you die during the period, or term, that the insurance is in force. For example, a term policy of $50,000 for 10 years would pay your beneficiary $50,000 in the event you die anywhere in the period between when the policy becomes effective (generally the date you apply for insurance, or the date you are approved by the insurance company) and ten years from that date. If you have a policy that became effective 10/1/2009 for ten years, it would cover you for the period up to 10/1/2019. If you become ill on 9/20/2019 and die on 10/4/2019, you collect nothing. If you are healthy until you die on 10/2/2019, you collect nothing. You need to die during the term of the insurance to collect.

Also, the insurance is in effect as long as you pay the premiums during the term of the insurance. (If you stop paying, your coverage ceases.) Term policies do not have a cash value, or reserve, to cover future premiums. Everything you pay in the way of premium goes to cover the cost of the insurance. It does not build value over time, and is only in force as long as you keep it in force. It is the form of insurance needing the least cash outlay.

If you wish to continue the insurance at the end of the term, there may be a provision, but the rate will be astronomically high—it will reflect the estimates from ten or twenty years ago (whenever you took out the policy) of what they thought the rate would be for someone 10 or 20 years older. Since more recent term insurance policies have had a lower cost of insurance than older policies, it you would probably get a better rate by just applying for a new policy (assuming you were healthy enough to qualify). Term insurance has a lower premium than permanent, but before you buy it, you need to be sure that:

- you won't need it for longer than the term covered, and
- you invest the savings to get as good a return as you would get with a permanent policy (see below).

Permanent insurance is a term used to describe a broad range of other types of policies. Despite its name, it is only permanent as long as there are funds available to pay the cost of insurance; it will lapse when the funds you've paid in, plus the dividends you've earned, run out.

If it is properly funded, it sticks around until you actually die, so your heirs always collect the death benefit. That is why it is called permanent. It also builds cash value over time. This is why I call it "life and death" insurance. If you decide you don't want the policy anymore, you get back the cash value. You also can borrow against the cash value. Pay premiums for a long enough period of time, and you'll have a pile of money you can use, tax-free, to spend any way you wish, to enhance your life. Plus, you'll have the death benefit when you die. Money for living, plus money at death.

It is **designed** to last until you die. (Whether or not it lasts depends on how well it was designed, and how well the investment portion of the policy performs.) A portion of the premium you pay is used to pay the cost of insurance (which is what the premium of a term policy would be used for). The balance of the premium is invested by the insurance company, and builds a value that you have access to. Each year, a portion of the premium you pay in that year goes to cover the cost of insurance, and the rest gets added to the investment pool. Ideally, over time, this invested portion grows significantly.

At some point in time, the annual cost of insurance will have increased so that it is greater than the premium you are paying. At that time, the difference is taken from the invested portion. If the growth in the invested portion increases greater than the amount that is taken out to cover the premium, the investment will continue to grow. If not, the investment will gradually decrease.

There are many variations on this type of life insurance. In the 1990's everyone got excited about variable life insurance, and universal life insurance. Most people who bought variable are sorry—it did not live up to its expectations. Universal has some good attributes, and is appropriate for some situations, but I usually stay away from it. (One notable exception is certain policies used as a substitute for long term care insurance, but there are very few of these. See **LIST #11: Three Facts You Need to Know About Aging** for details.)

My preference is for cash value whole life insurance, purchased from:

- a mutual life insurance company,
- which offers competitive premiums
- and a strong dividend paying history.

In my opinion, it is the best value for your money. I own a lot of it.

MISTAKE #2: Death insurance is expensive (but looks cheap) and is usually a waste of money.

Term insurance (death insurance) has a lower annual premium than permanent insurance. That's why it looks cheap. It actually makes sense in some cases, such as when you don't have any cash, and you need insurance for a short period of time for a specific purpose. But most term insurance policies never pay out a claim. People either drop the policy, or live too long. Over 98% of the policies never pay a claim. That's why insurance companies love them—they are pure profit. The reason term insurance ends up being expensive is that you are just throwing the money away. Plus, the money you spent could have been growing for you in an investment. So there is an opportunity cost. You could have been making money with the premiums you paid.

Properly planned permanent insurance will cause you to pay more out of pocket each year than term will, but eventually it can pay you back every penny you put in, with interest, while you are alive, plus, leave a substantial sum to your heirs on your death. In other words, you can make money with permanent insurance. And since everyone dies eventually, it always pays out, as long as you keep it going.

MISTAKE #3: Most people insure themselves against the losses that are least likely to occur, and don't insure against the most likely losses. And they wait too long to get the right insurance.

What type of insurance policies do you have? Most likely, you have automobile insurance. But the odds of getting into anything bigger than a fender bender are low. You probably have homeowner's insurance or renter's insurance, but the odds of your home burning down, or all your possessions stolen, are extremely low. You most likely have health insurance, but the chances of a major hospitalization are small.

So what is likely? Chances are high that you will be unable to work at some point in your life, due to a temporary or permanent disability. But very few people have disability insurance.

Chances are greater than 40% for men and 60% for women that you will need some form of long-term care in your old age, but most people don't have long-term care insurance.

And there is a 100% chance that you will die, sometime. But most people who die don't have permanent life insurance.

Why would you spend money to protect yourself from something that is not likely to occur, and not spend money for something that is much more likely to occur, or for something that will certainly occur?

When people finally figure out the correct insurance to get, they have generally already wasted away decades. They've lost the chance to have their money compound for a long period of time, and the insurance component of their premium, as compared to the investment component, is high.

For example, I recently wrote policies on a 15 year old male child and a 44 year old female parent. The policies were for the same amount of coverage. His premium was $2,500 a year. Hers was $7,600 a year. Both had the same cash values in 30 years. She just committed to spending the difference in the two premiums ($4,600 a year) for 30 years, or $127,000 extra, to get the same result in cash value and insurance coverage. That's because she waited to buy until she was in her mid-forties.

Everybody asks me when the proper time to buy long term care insurance is. The answer is: ideally, you want to buy it one day before you qualify for benefits, while you are healthy enough to still get coverage at a good rate. Obviously, I'm being facetious, but it shows why there is no correct answer to that question. You can buy it while you are very young, and pay premiums for years with little likelihood of needing the coverage before you are 65, or you can wait until your early 50's, when the annual cost of waiting starts to sharply increase. But there's a danger to waiting. Everyone forgets this: by your early 50's, you've probably been to the doctor sufficient times, and have had enough tests run, so that are indicators of what your health will be down the road. You already know your blood pressure and cholesterol levels. You've had a colonoscopy. You've done a stress test. If you're susceptible to kidney stones, you know it. And because insurance companies get to see your medical records, they know the same things you do. And more. Remember, when people are being evaluated for long-term care, the insurance company doesn't look to see if you will die young or old, as they do with life insurance. They only care about one thing: how poor will your health be in the years preceding your death, and how long will you linger in poor health? I have a booklet one insurance company publishes, which list 426 possible ailments. If your medical records contain a diagnosis of any of 168 of these diseases, they will not write you a long-term care insurance policy. Now some of these diseases are extremely rare, so it is not exactly a 1/3 chance that you will be uninsurable, but there also are another hundred or so diseases that make the cost of insurance go up. By waiting, you increase the chances that you will not be insurable, or insurable only at a higher price. The booklet also lists 308 medications. If you take one or more of 84 of them, you're also uninsurable by some companies.

Usually, we can find some insurance, at any age, but it may be limited in coverage, or more than you want to pay.

Don't wait to buy insurance for what is likely or certain to occur. Buy it now, when it is less expensive, and obtainable.

MISTAKE #4: Most people don't understand the insurance they buy.

They did not ask the right questions, and the sales person did not tell them the right questions to ask. Make sure that you understand what you are buying, and that it is clearly explained to you. If the salesperson cannot explain the policy to you, get a different salesperson. If you cannot find what you are told in print, or you do not understand what you are reading, and it cannot be explained to you, return the policy, and get a different policy, a different salesperson, or both.

MISTAKE #5: Nobody reads the sales literature and the policy. Be the exception. Avoid free meals.

I don't know why people don't read the sales literature and the insurance policies. It is all written out in plain English, with lots of examples. Insurance is one of the most highly regulated industries in the U.S. You have to sign a lot of documents before you get a policy. Everything has to be clearly explained in writing. You never have to rely on anything that is not in writing.

If people read the sales literature and policies, and made the salesperson explain clearly everything they did not understand, fewer people would end up with the wrong policies. If people made a point of not listening to anything they were told, and just read the sales material and polices, they wouldn't make mistakes. If your salesperson can't explain the sales material to you, or find someone who can—work with a different salesperson.

How do you know if you understand correctly what you've bought? Repeat it to someone else—a friend, a spouse, a co-worker. If they understand what you say, you're okay.

I live in Miami. It's the senior citizen capital of the world, and the scam capital of the world. It's the home of the early bird meal. It is still the only place in the world where Sweet 'n Low packets are available only by request, because if they were left on the tables, they'd be pocketed by thrifty diners. It's the only major city where $1 admission movie theaters, which sell tokens to put in turnstiles to admit patrons to the theater, are plagued by an epidemic of slugs, used by patrons who are trying to see a movie for less than a buck. FREE is the most compelling sales pitch, and the only people cleverer than those who take advantage of FREE things are those who use FREE to ensnare and scam the less than fully wary. I am constantly being offered free meals to listen to financial sales pitches.

I found this on-line, as part of a press release being issued by a law firm. I don't know what their source is, but the information could be true:

"A recent investigation by the SEC of 110 "free lunch" seminars found...deficiency letters or letters of caution were sent to 78% of the investment firms...23%...are under review for possible further investigation by ...SEC." No surprise.

In and of themselves, free meals are not bad. You can learn things. You might even enjoy the meal (but not the persistent post-meal phone calls). But you won't get investment advice that is right for you, at the meal.

Here's why: What you will be presented with is generic advice, which touts the investments that are the most profitable to the sellers. What you need is something tailored to your specific needs. There's no "one size fits all" in financial products. There's an old saying that you have two ears and one mouth, and two eyes and one heart. Two ears and one mouth means that you should listen twice as much as you talk. At these free seminars, you don't get to talk at all, and no one is listening to you. Two eyes and one heart means that you should use one eye to see the goodness in others, and the other the faults in yourself. Too often you meet people who use one to see the faults in you, and the other to see the opportunities they have to sell you something inappropriate for you, but profitable for them.

You don't need free meals to get information. You have the Internet. Check out anything you want to know online.

If you do want to use a financial advisor, give them the information they need to customize a proposal for you. Make them back it up with data. Then check out the answers on the Internet. Get someone else to review the proposal and pick it apart. Make the advisor explain it to you in his or her own words, without referring to the sales literature. You'll quickly determine who you want your advisor to be.

Also, don't hesitate to ask the advisor what they are being paid on any product they sell you. Don't be alarmed by high numbers—financial products pay high commissions and fees. It takes a huge amount of time for a financial advisor to learn about the products available, stay current with the market, plan for your needs, and put the right plans in place. Do be alarmed when the salesperson cannot explain why the product is good for you despite the fees. I tell my clients that the best product for them to buy is usually the least rewarding one for me to sell, because when I make less, more of their premium goes to work for them.

Obviously, the conflict between what is best for the client and what benefits the advisor most has the potential for bad results with the ethically challenged salesperson. Some people try to avoid this by getting advice from an advisor who is compensated by a flat fee, and not a commission, and buying the products elsewhere. That can work. But if you go that route, you are still going to buy a product in the end from someone who earns a commission, so you need to get both a good fee based advisor, and a properly motivated salesperson. You still also need to avoid uneducated or unethical commission based salespeople.

The real solution is to know who you are buying from, and getting clear answers to your questions.

My short recommendation in choosing an advisor is the 4 "C's", similar to the grading scale used in the diamond industry. But my "C's" are different. They are:

- **Care**—Your insurance agent must care about you. He or she must listen well, so that the two of you can jointly assess your needs, and develop an appropriate plan together. Your agent must be able to learn enough about you, by listening and by asking questions, to make appropriate recommendations.
- **Confidentiality**—You will be discussing sensitive financial and personal medical data. You need to be comfortable that the person you are sharing this with—your agent—will respect this confidentiality.
- **Connections**—Insurance is complex and diverse. No one person can have all the expertise needed for all situations. In choosing an agent, you need to select someone who is well connected, who has affiliations and resources to draw upon to answer the multitude of questions that will come up.
- **Compatibility**—Do you feel comfortable talking to your agent? Is this someone you respect? Buying insurance is not a "sales" process—you should not be "sold" something by a "salesperson." It is a **partnership** between you and someone who has your needs at heart, and someone who can work with you to jointly arrive at good decisions with you.

For more discussion on what to look for, see **LIST #4: Nine Qualities to Look for in a Financial Advisor**.

MISTAKE #6: People pay premiums monthly.

This is foolish. The additional charge for paying monthly instead of annually can range from 5% to 20% a year, or higher. Why would you want to pay crazy interest rates like that? It is almost always going to be less expensive for you to borrow money someplace else, and pay premiums annually. Not sure how much your monthly premiums are costing you? Read the policy. It is stated explicitly in there. Don't have enough money to pay the annual premium all at once? I don't care—beg, borrow, or scrape the funds together. Then, the next month, put one-twelfth of the annual premium in a savings account, and do the same every month. Forget it is there. Never take any money from that account, except when you get your premium notice. This way, you'll have the next premium that is due, and you can start the process all over again.

MISTAKE #7: Most people set up their retirement plans so that they'll run out of money before they die.

Not on purpose, of course. They just don't think it through. If you retire in your mid-sixties, you need to plan on 25-30 years of retirement income. Of that time period, last few years will have an additional expense associated with it, for assistance with the routine tasks of daily living. You may need to have someone coming into your home for a few hours a week or day, or you may be going to an adult day care center, or you may permanently relocate to an assisted facility or nursing home. It will most likely start out with occasional help, building to full-time as you age. In today's dollars, it could easily run $4,000 to $8,000 a month extra (for full-time care).

Most people don't plan for any of this. Because it is not pleasant to think about. But the future is going to happen, whether you plan for it or not. The only difference will be your lifestyle.

The bulk of this book is devoted to lists on how to prepare for retirement, and long term care. Read them.

MISTAKE #8: People complain about taxes, but ignore the opportunities to avoid taxes, legally.

There are three ways to handle taxes: now, later, or never.

"Now" means income taxes, sales taxes, excise taxes (gasoline, tobacco, alcohol, etc.) No way to avoid these, unless you can defer some of the income taxes.

"Later" is deferred taxes—income put into an IRA or an annuity, reinvesting proceeds of a sale, etc. You hope that you'll be in a lower tax bracket when you need to pay taxes on this income.

"Never" is income that you get tax-free. Like the proceeds on life insurance payouts. Or the cash accumulation in life insurance policies that you take out.

Want a hint on the best way to deal with taxes? Think about this: Six of the largest U.S. banks report that they have more money invested in life insurance than they do in branches, real estate, fixed assets, etc. Because they know that they are going to make more money on the payout of life insurance on key employees, tax-free, than they will on any other asset. (Source: Medical Economics, June 19, 2009.) Life insurance can play an important part of your program for financial security, wealth preservation, and retirement. It is mentioned in nearly every list in this book. Read them. Whole life insurance with cash value is the best way to earn money tax free, legally, with certainty. Learn about it.

SUMMARY: How do you avoid making these mistakes?

The insurance world is complex, obscure, and hard to understand.

A good agent has a solid team behind him or her—good companies, strong staff support, excellent resources to call on.

The plan your brother-in-law has will most likely not work for you. You need to work with someone who understands your particular situation. You need to work with someone who can talk clearly about the different types of products, and why they are or are not appropriate for you. You need to work with someone who is comfortable working with all your other financial advisors. You are only going to get one shot to set up a good plan that will fund your lifestyle for as long as you live. Most likely, you'll want the best advice you can get. You can buy the same insurance and other assets from anyone, at the same prices. What you cannot shop is the expertise, the integrity, and the level of care that the top advisors provide.

See MISTAKE #5 above to learn about the 4 "C's" of choosing an insurance advisor. See **LIST #4: Nine Qualities to Look for in a Financial Advisor** for more details.

"Saved for college for the kids—not retirement."

LIST 7: EIGHT RULES FOR PREPARING FOR THE FUTURE (FINANCIAL SECURITY IN RETIREMENT)

RULE #1: Have more money coming in than going out, either through passive income, such as investments, or earnings.

If the combination of your earned income and investment income does not meet your expenses, either increase income or cut expenses. It is usually possible to do both, but it is easier to cut expenses that than to earn more income. It is generally possible, however, to increase UNEARNED income by investing smarter.

EXCEPTION TO RULE 1: If you are "retired" (i.e., not actively earning much income because you are older), it is OK to spend more than is coming in, IF and ONLY IF you have sufficient assets to GUARANTEE that you will not run out of money, ever, before you die. (See **LIST 10: I'm Retired, Now What?**)

RULE #2: Protect your income, either from loss due to disability, or from not working.

There are absolutely no reliable numbers that predict loss of income due to accident or disability by age or occupation, due to wildly varying factors, and inflated claims by people trying to cheat the system. All we know for sure is that you have a greater chance of being disabled than you do of dying if you are under 67. We're going to look at disability insurance, also known as paycheck insurance, in detail in **LIST #12: Paycheck Insurance (Keeping Your Paycheck Coming When You Can't Go to Work)**. But here's a good way to start estimating what your needs might be if you are disabled:

1. Determine how much EARNED income you need to run your household on a break-even basis.

2. Determine how this would change if some or all of your earned income stopped before age 67, either permanently, or for a limited period of time. Include in your calculations:

    a. Decrease in expenses if you are not working (lunch out, work clothes, unreimbursed auto or travel, lower cell phone costs, reduced child care because you are home more, etc.).

    b. Additional expenses you'd expect from being disabled (caretaker, more medical supplies not covered by insurance, extended rehab, etc.).

    c. Other sources of income you would have if you are disabled, but not included above (financial support from family, friends, etc.; current insurance from work; income you could earn while disabled).

3. Figure out how much monthly disability insurance you need by combining the above results. This should be called paycheck insurance, but it's not. It means that

you need to have insurance that will bring in the same amount as your net paycheck, if you are disabled.

4. Decide how many months you can wait until disability insurance kicks in, either by using savings, quickly selling assets, borrowing, etc. Don't forget to factor in any short-term disability insurance you may have from work. Use this to select the elimination period on your disability policy.

5. Determine how much money you would need if you quit and started job hunting, or if you had a period of time between leaving one job and starting another. Take into account both voluntary and forced non-income producing periods. Also consider temporary reductions in income due to cutbacks, unpaid time off for pleasure or to handle an emergency. Add in funds for unusual increased expenses, such uninsured losses (deductibles on auto, home, renter, health etc. insurances; emergency funds for you or someone else, etc.)

6. The combination of the funds for a disability elimination period and emergencies plus job interruption is what you need to have readily available—cash, checking accounts, easily disposed of collectibles (gold and jewelry), highest quality stocks that don't fluctuate much under adverse conditions (if such stocks still exist), bonds, CD's, etc.

7. If you don't have enough of these assets, your 2nd goal, after insuring your income due to disability, is to accumulate these assets quickly.

RULE #3: Once you have protected your income while you are working, plan on how you will live when you retire, even if that is decades off.

You need to consider 2 scenarios:

The first scenario is for while you are retired and still healthy. You need to start accumulating assets now that will produce income later. This can be investments, real estate, your home, insurance, IRA's, 401k's, retirement accounts, annuities, businesses, collectibles—anything that will endure after you stop working, grow in value over the years, and produce income, or that can be sold (over time) to produce cash.

The second scenario is for when you are retired and not in good health. You need to put in place a FAILSAFE system that will cover expenses above and beyond those needed for when you are healthy. I call this "income assistance for the expenses of aging," because it is like disability insurance, except it starts when traditional disability insurance stops (usually retirement or age 67.) Of course, this old age insurance does not have to be a traditional insurance policy—if you've accumulated sufficient assets so that you can sell them off as you need funds AND NEVER RUN OUT. This acts as your old age "disability" insurance.

GOOD NEWS and BAD NEWS about RULE #3:

The good news is that you can plan now so that some assets will work for you whether you age well or poorly. The same money put away now can work for you in either case, and as you move from good health to poor.

The bad news is that the younger you are, the less you know about what you will have available to you in the future, and so you have to make a lot of wild guesses, and plan around them. It can drive you crazy. You don't know how much money you are going to make in your lifetime, how well your investments will perform, whether or not you will be disabled, and how long you will stay healthy after retirement.

There is one factor, however, that still lets you plan intelligently for part of the future, and that is actuarial prediction, which is this:

No one knows what will happen to you, personally. But mathematicians can predict, with stunning accuracy, what will happen to a large group of people who resemble you. Take a large enough group of people your age, your gender, your lifestyle, your current state of health, and they can predict, accurately:

- How many will die every year for the next 120 years
- How many will be disabled or need help due to aging in each of the next 120 years

If enough people in your group pool sufficient funds (insurance premiums) and they give it to someone to manage wisely (insurance companies), there will be sufficient funds available over the next 120 years to pay an agreed upon amount when each person dies (term life insurance) or gets disabled or needs old age help (disability and long term care insurance). Furthermore, if this group puts in more than the minimum amount needed to pay out claims, these will be a sufficient pool of extra money that can be accessed temporarily as needed (cash value life insurance) or paid in advance of when benefits would ordinarily be received, or when you meet certain criteria that show that you are likely to live a shorter period of time (accelerated benefits on life insurance).

Using insurance products, correctly purchased, lets you avoid the bad consequences of RULE #3. (But we'll go into that more after the other rules are outlined.) Obeying RULE

#3 is more important than obeying RULE #4. You also want to pay attention to **LIST #11: Three Facts You Need to Know About the Cost of Aging (Long Term Care).**

RULE #4: Amass as much wealth as you can to fund expenses in the years when expenses exceed income (private school, college, large purchases, unexpected and uninsured expenses, weddings, huge vacations, periodic splurges on luxuries).

But always remember, RULE #3 is MORE IMPORTANT than RULE #4. This is because everything in RULE #4 is optional:

If you can't afford schooling, there will be subsidies and loans.

If you can't afford large weddings, you'll have small ones.

If you can't afford large purchases, such as cars, boats, second homes, vacations, you'll do without.

If you can't cover the expense of the roof blowing off your house, you'll cover the holes with a tarp.

Etc.

But RULE #3 is not optional.

If you do not have enough money to live your lifestyle in health or sickness, after you retire, you will be dependent on your children, the government, and charity. Your lifestyle will be different than you planned, the severity of the change may shorten your life, and the conditions may be unpleasant. And you have no way of knowing for certain the ability and willingness of your relatives, the government, and charity to pitch in.

The good parts of RULES #3 and #4 is that the earlier you start planning for #3, the less expensive it will be, so you'll have more available for #4. And anything above what you've spent by age 67 automatically rolls over into more for retirement.

RULE #5: While amassing wealth, only put at risk that which you are willing to lose.

This is a no brainer, but most people ignore it and this impedes their accumulation of wealth.

Any investment you make has risk. Anything you buy, you can lose. Nothing is 100% safe or 100% sure. Some risks are innocuous, with limited potential for loss, and a lot to gain. Buying an occasional lottery ticket for $1 now and then is unlikely to change your lifestyle—you'll probably find a way to gain this back by cutting an expense somewhere else, and you could win a million bucks. Highly unlikely, but possible, and it only costs $1.

But we also gamble with every other financial decision we make, and the larger the amount we put at risk, and the greater the type of risk, the more it slows down our efforts to amass wealth.

It sounds obvious. We should be able to accurately assess risk and reward, but we're only human, so we usually err.

RULE #6: Protect your wealth.

Whatever you amass, make sure it is protected against loss. The four primary causes of loss, and their antidotes are:

1—Natural occurrences. Weather damage, health damage, theft, accident, etc. Protect yourself by having insurance for anything that is at risk, by staying fit, by being careful.

2—Economic and financial occurrences. Communal economic downturns, personal economic downturns (like job loss). Protect yourself with insurance and a safety net, and minimize risk to wealth you've amassed.

3—Malfeasance and theft. Understand all the risks associated with everything you do. Don't rely on others to manage your assets—help is fine; abdication is not. Insure against loss. Carry umbrella insurance against large, unusual claims. Keep assets in trusts, not individual names. This provides added protection against others spending your money foolishly, and protects it from civil judgments.

RULE #7: Structure your assets so that you can enjoy the benefit of having them while you are alive and healthy.

Look for things to own that let you use them while they grow in value. Avoid assets that you merely get to "wave at." Huge balances in investment accounts don't benefit you if you cannot access the income to fund your lifestyle. Avoid putting funds in the wrong "buckets" so that you do not take from the wrong bucket at the wrong time. See LIST #8 and LIST #9 for a fuller discussion of "buckets."

RULE #8: Structure your assets so that you never have to sell any of them at the wrong time, if things do not go according to plan.

This is the most important one of all, once you've accumulated some assets. This is the essence of the "buckets" philosophy.

LIST 8: OVER THE HILL (HEALTH CARE, INCOME, LIQUIDITY, LEGACY)—KEY ISSUES YOU NEED TO ADDRESS BEFORE YOU GET OLD

If you are under the age of 50, you are not going to believe anything I tell you in this LIST, unless you are brighter than 95% of your peers.

If you are between ages 50 and 60, what I have to say may sound vaguely probable, but you probably think it doesn't apply to you.

If you are over 60, and you haven't read this before, you'll be kicking yourself, because what I am saying is blatantly true, obvious to all senior citizens who read it, yet implemented by few.

This is the message:

If you are under 60 years old today and in decent health, you stand a good chance of living until your 90's. This means that you can live 30 years or more past your wage earning days, and you probably won't feel "old" until the last few years of your life. Your health will be pretty good, until it gradually declines, and then you'll deteriorate to death over the last 3 to 5 years of your life. Suddenly, it will become very expensive for you to be taken care of.

Yet most people do not plan to have a secure, large enough, base of assets by the time they stop working, to provide enough to live on for the rest of their lives.

Even more do not plan for the added expenses of aging badly.

And that means the quality of your declining years will not be what you want it to be.

Here's why:

Health Care:

Medicare and Medicaid are going to change from what we have today—it is too expensive for the government to provide the programs that currently exist, and there are too few people funding it. It is mathematically impossible for the government to pay as much as it currently does for each retiree, especially now that the baby boomers are retiring, and the work force is shrinking.

The only thing working in the government's favor is a two-edged sword—obesity. So many Americans are so out of shape and overweight that life expectancies will probably go down before they go up. The good news for the government is that there will be fewer old people to take care of. The bad news is that their last years will be more expensive, as they consume more and more ineffective medical care. (On the other hand, they won't have that many bad years—their bodies just won't last that long.) Don't take my word for it— hang out in a hospital lobby, and see the condition of patients who are being discharged. Then look at the people who came to take them home, or go around the corner and sit in the emergency room lobby, and see what brings them in. Next, go to the airport, and count the number of people who won't comfortably fit into the seats they will be sitting in for the next few hours. The airlines have spent so much time worrying about the excessive size of the luggage you are attempting to carry on, that they have totally ignored the excessive size of the people they are trying to cram into rows of 3 and 4 across.

If you have not planned for the added expenses of aging poorly, you are doomed to a poor lifestyle in old age. See **LIST 11: Three Facts You Need to Know About the Cost of Aging (Long Term Care).**

But what is the cost of basic medical care in retirement? What type of government sponsored health insurance are you going to have in retirement, how much will it cost, and what will it cover? Forgive me if I cannot give you a precise number on what to budget. It's a long way off, and medical costs do not follow other cost trends. If you want to be safe, figure $10,000 to $15,000 out of pocket per year, per person, plus inflation, plus rising costs. Times two, for a couple. Then times 30 years, since it is not unreasonable to assume that you and your spouse could live to age 95.

How do you plan for this, especially since we don't know the rates Congress will set for Medicare premiums?

Ideally, you want to create a private pension plan to fund basic medical costs. You do this by investing a sum of money, now, which will be able to throw off $15,000 to $30,000 a year when you retire, and continue doing so for 30 years or more. The two strongest options for doing this are life insurance (the kind with cash value, usually called "whole life"), and annuities.

This is more important than long term care, college educations, and legacies. The only thing more important is having enough money for living expenses.

The cost and nature or medical care in retirement raises basic questions and concerns, so you would think that they should have basic answers, but that's not the case at all. In fact, medical care plans in retirement are more complicated than coverage provided by employer sponsored plans while you are working—it's a trick the system plays on people who are getting on in years—we make it harder for them to figure out what is appropriate for them, at a time when their mental skills are starting to decline.

Given this confusion and lack of knowledge, it is not surprising that many people underestimate their medical expenses in retirement, and hence do not budget for it correctly. Add to that the uncertainty of what medical costs will be in the future (I've heard 4% to 6.3% cited as today's average annual increase), and you can see why planning for medical care in retirement is difficult.

During working years, most people have either an employer sponsored health plan, an individual plan, or no health insurance coverage at all. (I'm skipping Medicaid, which is for people below the poverty line.) If you continue working beyond age 65, you may have the option to continue with your employer sponsored health plan, and, depending on how much the employer pays and the quality of the plan, that may be the best option for you. Most people, however, working or not, go on Medicare.

Medicare Part A (also known as Original Medicare) is automatic. You turn 65, and you are automatically enrolled. For most people, there is no monthly premium—it is covered by the payments you made into the system while you were working. (Naturally, there are some exceptions—such as if you have not paid Medicare taxes through employment. Also, some disabilities get you Medicare at an earlier age. And some diseases, and railroad workers, are treated differently. In some cases, if you are not covered, you may be able to purchase Part A.) Medicare Part A covers PART of the following:

- hospital stays
- skilled nursing facility stays
- hospice
- home health care.

It does NOT cover all of the costs for these. It does NOT cover ANY costs for long term care or custodial care. There IS a deductible. You can pretty much count on paying over $1,000 per person per year before coverage kicks in.

Medicare Part B is optional. You can purchase it only if you are eligible for Part A. It covers PART of the following costs:

- doctors' services and visits
- outpatient care
- some home health care
- some preventive services
- some tests and therapy
- ambulance services
- rehab or physical therapy
- flu shots
- colorectal cancer screenings.

There is a monthly premium, which is deducted from your Social Security benefits check. The cost varies—it depends on income, when you sign up, and a variety of other factors. There is a deductible. And there is a co pay. It is possible to pay thousands of dollars a year, per person, on premiums, deductibles, and co pays for Part B.

Then there are Medicare Part C plans. These are offered privately, not by the government, but they are regulated by the government. There are more than a dozen different plans, and prices vary, depending on plan, and location. They are also called Medicare Advantage plans. They replace Parts A and B, and sometimes include some drug coverage. Medicare Advantage Plans can save you money, since out-of-pocket costs in these plans are generally lower than with Original Medicare alone. But each Medicare Advantage Plan can charge different out of pocket costs, and have different rules

for how you get services (like whether you need a referral to
see a specialist or if you have to go to only doctors, facilities,
or suppliers that belong to the plan). They come in many
flavors, including:

- PPO
- HMO
- private fee for service
- special needs plans
- medical savings account plans.

There are time limits when you can sign up for them, and
some restrictions—you are not eligible, for instance, if you are
on dialysis for end stage kidney disease.

If you decide you don't want Part C, but still want
additional coverage over and beyond what Parts A & B
provide, you can purchase Medigap, or supplemental private
insurance, which covers all or some of the costs not covered
by Parts A & B. Again, costs and coverage vary widely, and
it is a chore to figure out if you are better off with a Part C
Advantage plan, or a supplemental plan. The challenge,
basically, is to figure out what will cost you less, between co
pays and deductibles, and premiums, and often you won't
know the answer until you start receiving services, and getting
bills. This mutual exclusivity (you cannot have Part A–Original
Medicare–and a Medical Advantage plan, and you cannot
have a Medical Advantage plan and a Medigap plan) has
been a major source of fraud and fraudulent enrollments
by unscrupulous agents, and often results in the cancelling
of coverage that you really want to have. It is very confusing.
You cannot have a Medigap and a Medicare Supplement plan
at the same time. Also, not all plans are offered in all states,
and while the plans are labeled with letter (i.e., Plan F), the
meaning of the letters differs in certain states.

Be prepared to spend thousands of dollars a year on premiums, or services that you need to pay for because you do not have Part C, or a substitute.

Lastly, there is Part D, which covers some drugs, and some of the costs. If you don't sign up when you are first eligible, it may cost more to join later. And there are gaps in coverage, and deductibles. You can pay additional thousands of dollars a year, or more, plus premiums, if you have Part D, (and more if you don't.)

All in all, you need to budget something like $10,000 to $12,000 a year for medical care in retirement, or after age 65, depending on what services you use. These are today's numbers. And because there are so many possible plans and usage levels, these numbers can vary. And, this is just for regular care like you get from insurance while you are working. This does NOT include long term care.

By the way, dental is not covered by Medicare unless it is part of something else, like repairing your mouth after cancer surgery, for instance. Hearing and vision are also not covered. You need separate budgets for these expenses.

Income:

We're coming out of a rough decade of up and down investment returns, and going in to more of the same. The difference between us and our parents is that we're generally self-managing our retirement portfolios, whereas our parents had their retirement sewed up in company pensions, private retirement plans, and other retirement vehicles. Over 70% of Americans are planning on retiring with Social Security alone. This means that there will be more and more retirees greeting you at Wal-Mart due to their need to supplement income. You need to save now to plan for a guaranteed income of sufficient amounts of money to afford the lifestyle you want to live. See my **LIST #9: Income Security in Retirement**.

Liquidity:

This is also known as the "buckets" theory.

It is very basic.

Over your lifetime, you are going to amass various kinds of financial assets. You may have:

- annuities
- businesses
- stocks
- real estate
- cash
- gold and jewelry
- IRA's and retirement accounts
- collectibles
- bonds
- CD's
- inheritances
- cash value life insurance
- trusts
- primary and secondary homes
- other investments.

These are your "buckets."

Very few of these are liquid at any one time: Real estate takes time to sell, and the market has to be right. Precious metals are easier to sell, but the market has to be right. CD's are easy to sell, but if you cash them in early, you can lose money. Annuities have withdrawal penalties for taking money out too soon. Insurance is generally a long-term affair. Stocks are easily converted to cash, but timing is everything.

The key is to have "defensive" buckets and "offensive" buckets.

Defensive buckets are the ones that are minimally fluctuating, easily convertible to cash, and don't have penalties to access early. Think cash, short-term bonds, cash value of life insurance, older annuities.

Offensive buckets are the ones that are going to grow, eventually, but that you may not be able to touch at certain times, such as when their value is down. Think stocks, real estate, investments, gold.

The key is to balance your offensive and defensive investments so that you never have to dip into the wrong bucket at the wrong time.

It's that simple.

Keep it all balanced, and make sure that you always have enough in the buckets so you will not cause you a loss if you need to convert to cash and draw funds out. Make sure you have funds in your defensive buckets that you can access to live on when your offensive buckets are low.

Never dip into the wrong bucket at the wrong time. You don't want to be selling stocks, when they are down, to pull out funds for living expenses—you want your annuity payments to handle that. You don't want to be depleting buckets that you need to grow if you are short on cash—that is what the cash value of life insurance is for. You don't want to be selling investments that you are counting on to produce income.

Legacy:

Dying is expensive, and it generally happens at the wrong time, financially.

If you haven't planned properly, estate taxes, or income taxes on tax-deferred assets, like IRA's, can eat up your legacy.

Unpleasant as it is to think about, you are better off planning while you are alive, than letting your heirs deal with a mess after you pass. Remember, everyone has an estate plan. Some of us have one that we planned for ourselves, and the rest of us have the one that the government planned without asking us. Which one do you want to have?

"Spent it all on the kids—figured the government would take care of
old age."

LIST 9: INCOME SECURITY IN RETIREMENT

Many people look at income for retirement and think "annuities" or "investment accounts." But that is only part of the picture.

Deferred annuities are a way to put money in an account, and have it grow tax-deferred until you start taking money out. The catch is that you cannot take money out of deferred annuities, without paying a penalty, before age 59 ½, and you must take required minimum distributions from tax-deferred annuities after age 70 ½. You can use IRA's or 401k money to fund an annuity, or you can use after-tax (non-qualified) money to fund the annuity.

If you use IRA money, you pay income taxes on everything when you withdraw the funds in retirement, since you did not pay income tax on the funds you contributed.

If you use non-qualified money to fund the annuity, you only pay income tax on the gains when you withdraw funds, and not the entire amount—you already paid taxes on the initial funds put in.

You can put unlimited funds into an annuity, either all at once, or over time.

Immediate annuities have greater flexibility on payout, and no age related penalties, but they lack some ability to grow over time, because you start taking money out immediately.

Fixed or variable annuities can be an important part of a retirement strategy.

Fixed annuities provide a stream of income that is guaranteed for life, or for a period that you choose, (or a combination of the two) based on the amount you put in initially, the promised fixed rate of growth, and your age at the date your want to start receiving income. There are no surprises. There are also indexed fixed annuities, which provide some upside potential for the income, while guaranteeing a base income. It is possible to add in death benefit features, for additional cost.

Variable annuities fluctuate in value, and the income stream will depend on the value when you start drawing income. More recent variable annuity products include guaranteed base benefits, guaranteed death benefits, and a lot of features that vary from product to product that make them more attractive. Some even give you unlimited opportunity to invest your funds with impunity, benefiting if the market selections you make prosper, but protecting you if you make bad decisions. There are also hybrid products—fixed guaranteed minimums, with the opportunity for growth if the market does well.

Both types of annuities let your money grow tax deferred until you start taking income. This means that it is easier to build an accumulation for you to use as a base for taking income in the future.

The downside is that fees for annuities can be steep. If the market goes up, you end up with less than you would have if you had invested in a variety of funds on your own. But the benefit is the guarantees—if you can live with the minimum promised income, you've saved yourself from worry, from managing funds in your old age, and from the prospect of running out of money. Annuities can also provide a death benefit—for a cost.

One thing you have to be careful of when comparing different types of investments and rates of return—you cannot average rates of return by themselves, and then apply them to results. It will not give you a mathematically correct result. You have to average the total returns, and then work backwards to get an average rate of return. Using returns averaged improperly can provide misleading results, and unscrupulous people use it to confuse you. For instance:

For example, let's say you invested $100, and got an 8.33% average return. You might assume that this means after 3 years, you would have $127.13:

Year	Start	Gain		End	% Gain
1	$ 100.00	$	8.33	$ 108.33	8.33%
2	$ 108.33	$	9.02	$ 117.35	8.33%
3	$ 117.35	$	9.77	**$127.13**	8.33%
Average					8.33%

Every year, your investment grew 8.33%, including growth on the income you earned in prior years. The total is three times 8.33 (25.00), divided by 3, for an average of 8.33%.

Now let's assume that there was not constant growth, but that the average was still 8.33%:

Year	% Gain
1	100%
2	-50%
3	-25%

The total also is 25% for the 3 years, for an average of 8.33% a year.

Now, let apply this second set of returns to the $100 investment:

Year	Start	Gain	End	% Gain
1	$ 100.00	$ 100.00	$ 200.00	100%
2	$ 200.00	$(100.00)	$ 100.00	-50%
3	$ 100.00	$ (25.00)	**$ 75.00**	-25%
Average				8.33%

With the same average 8.33%, you've actually lost money in 3 years! Instead of having $127.13 after three years, you have $75.00, which is less than you started with.

Now let's look at a longer period, and factoring in regular withdrawals: Start out with $500,000, and withdraw money every year. (Let's say we withdraw $30,000 the first year, and 3% more each following year.) In both scenarios below, you average 11.35% returns, but in one case, you end up with a balance, after 26 years, of $47,278, and in the other, $2,598,424! (This type of difference will be true for any investment account with varying returns.)

How is this possible?

	Portfolio 1				Portfolio 2		
Year	Investment Return	Withdrawal	Account Balance		Investment Return	Withdrawal	Account Balance
1	-8.35%	$30,000	$428,250		1.35%	$30,000	$476,750
2	4.05%	$30,900	$414,694		10.15%	$30,900	$494,240
3	14.35%	$31,827	$442,376		7.65%	$31,827	$500,222
4	19.05%	$32,782	$493,866		30.45%	$32,782	$619,758
5	-14.75%	$33,765	$387,256		-3.05%	$33,765	$567,091
6	-26.45%	$34,778	$250,049		31.55%	$34,778	$711,230
7	37.35%	$35,822	$307,620		16.85%	$35,822	$795,250
8	23.75%	$36,896	$343,784		5.25%	$36,896	$800,105
9	-7.25%	$38,003	$280,856		18.65%	$38,003	$911,321
10	6.65%	$39,143	$260,390		32.05%	$39,143	$1,164,256
11	18.65%	$40,317	$268,636		6.15%	$40,317	$1,195,541
12	32.15%	$41,527	$313,476		22.45%	$41,527	$1,422,413
13	-4.85%	$42,773	$255,499		21.15%	$42,773	$1,680,481
14	21.15%	$44,056	$265,481		-4.85%	$44,056	$1,554,921
15	22.45%	$45,378	$279,704		32.15%	$45,378	$2,009,450
16	6.15%	$46,739	$250,167		18.65%	$46,739	$2,337,474
17	32.05%	$48,141	$282,204		6.65%	$48,141	$2,444,775
18	18.65%	$49,585	$285,250		-7.25%	$49,585	$2,217,944
19	5.25%	$51,073	$249,153		23.75%	$51,073	$2,693,632
20	16.85%	$52,605	$238,530		37.35%	$52,605	$3,647,099
21	31.55%	$54,183	$259,603		-26.45%	$54,183	$2,628,258
22	-3.05%	$55,809	$195,876		-14.75%	$55,809	$2,184,781
23	30.45%	$57,483	$198,038		19.05%	$57,483	$2,543,499
24	7.65%	$59,208	$153,979		14.35%	$59,208	$2,849,283
25	10.15%	$60,984	$108,624		4.05%	$60,984	$2,903,695
26	1.35%	$62,813	**$47,278**		-8.35%	$62,813	**$2,598,424**
	11.35%	$1,156,590			11.35%	$1,156,590	
	Average	Total Withdrawn			Average	Total Withdrawn	

Look at the "Investment Return" column for each. You'll see that the numbers are the same, but in opposite order. For instance, in the first example, in Year 1, your return is -8.35% and in Year 26, it is +1.35%. In the second example, the numbers are reversed; Year 1 is up +1.35%, and Year 26 is down -8.35%. This pattern is repeated each subsequent year, and in each example, the money you withdraw is the same each year. (These are arbitrary numbers and do not reflect any actual performance.)

Obviously, the value of your investment is very sensitive to what happens each year in the market, and when you have positive and negative returns, so you cannot just take a general average of rates of return over time. The actual dollar value of any investment depends on what happens *each* year.

So if actual returns can vary so much depending on the *order* in which they occur, how do you use annuities or taxable investment accounts, but protect yourself in negative markets?

The answer is to combine these investments with cash value whole life insurance.

Annuities and investment accounts offer the opportunity for growth and income, but the timing of your withdrawals can affect account balances and future income. But by setting up an annuity or investment account, and coupling it a with permanent whole life insurance policy, you have the option to only take money from your annuity or investment account when the market is up. In down years, you can tap into the cash value of your life insurance, giving the annuity or investment account a chance to rebound. In up years, you can take income from your annuity or investment account, and let the cash value of your life insurance rebuild.

Let's look at combining whole life insurance and a rollover from an IRA into an annuity or an investment account.

Let's start at age 45. Assume you are putting money into an IRA or other tax-deferred account, and you also purchase a whole life insurance policy that has a cash value.

Now, fast forward to age 65, when you retire. Your IRA is worth $2,000,000, and you want to withdraw $150,000 a year, every year, to live on. (You only need $100,000 to live on, but we allow $50,000 to pay taxes on your withdrawals, assuming that you are in a 33% income tax bracket.)

The following chart shows what can happen if you invest $2,000,000 at age 65 and withdraw $150,000 every year. (The returns shown, by the way, are arbitrary, and do not represent anything that has happened, and are not a projection of what will happen. They are just one reasonable possibility of how varying up and down years might look.) At the end of 15 years, you would be left with $1,001,497—about half of your original amount.

Age	Beginning Balance	Withdrawal	After Withdrawal Balance	Return	End of Year Balance
65	$2,000,000	$150,000	$1,850,000	-14.60%	$1,579,900
66	1,579,900	150,000	$1,429,900	-26.30%	$1,053,836
67	1,053,836	150,000	$903,836	37.50%	$1,242,775
68	1,242,775	150,000	$1,092,775	23.90%	$1,353,948
69	1,353,948	150,000	$1,203,948	-7.10%	$1,118,468
70	1,118,468	150,000	$968,468	6.80%	$1,034,324
71	1,034,324	150,000	$884,324	18.80%	$1,050,576
72	1,050,576	150,000	$900,576	31.30%	$1,182,457
73	1,182,457	150,000	$1,032,457	-4.70%	$983,931
74	983,931	150,000	$833,931	21.30%	$1,011,559
75	1,011,559	150,000	$861,559	22.60%	$1,056,271
76	1,056,271	150,000	$906,271	6.30%	$963,366
77	963,366	150,000	$813,366	32.30%	$1,076,083
78	1,076,083	150,000	$926,083	18.80%	$1,100,187
79	1,100,187	$150,000	$950,187	5.40%	$1,001,497

Next, let's look at the same account, but showing you not taking any distributions after years where the market had a negative return (except where you had to, to meet IRS guidelines for required minimum distributions.) In this example, you do not take distributions at ages 66, 67, and 70, and only take a partial distribution at age 75. The net result is that after 15 years, your account has grown, not shrunk, and is now worth $3,356,013.

Age	Beginning Balance	Withdrawal	After Withdrawal Balance	Return	End of Year Balance
65	$2,000,000	$150,000	$1,850,000	-14.60%	$1,579,900
66	1,579,900	0	$1,579,900	-26.30%	$1,164,386
67	1,164,386	0	$1,164,386	37.50%	$1,601,031
68	1,601,031	150,000	$1,451,031	23.90%	$1,797,828
69	1,797,828	150,000	$1,647,828	-7.10%	$1,530,832
70	1,530,832	0	$1,530,832	6.80%	$1,634,928
71	1,634,928	150,000	$1,484,928	18.80%	$1,764,095
72	1,764,095	150,000	$1,614,095	31.30%	$2,119,307
73	2,119,307	150,000	$1,969,307	-4.70%	$1,876,749
74	1,876,749	**75,000**	$1,801,749	21.30%	$2,185,522
75	2,185,522	150,000	$2,035,522	22.60%	$2,495,550
76	2,495,550	150,000	$2,345,550	6.30%	$2,493,319
77	2,493,319	150,000	$2,343,319	32.30%	$3,100,212
78	3,100,212	150,000	$2,950,212	18.80%	$3,504,851
79	3,504,851	$150,000	$3,354,851	5.40%	$3,536,013

That's very nice. You are $2.35 million dollars ahead, 80 years old, and set for income for the next two decades. But what were you living on at ages 66, 67, 70 and 75?

Let's go back to when you were 65, and look at what had happened to the life insurance policy you had invested in at age 45 In this particular example, we look at a policy taken out for $1,000,000 at age 45 by a healthy male. The premium is $26,470, payable for 20 years. (This is a sample policy based on a blend of actual quotes—the actual numbers will vary depending on the insurance company, and the details of the policy, but this premium is a reasonable estimate of what such a policy could cost today.) By the time you reach age 65, you are done paying premiums, you've put in a total of $529,400 over the 20 years, and you have a cash value of $799,961 and a death benefit of $1,429,855.

	Whole Life Policy				Taxable Investment + Term Life		
Age Year End	Surrender Beg Yr.	Net Cash Value End Yr	Net Death Benefit End Yr		Withdrawals	Account Balance	Death Benefit
66	$0	$799,961	$1,429,855		$0	731,277	$0
67	100,000	740,997	1,291,835		100,000	652,425	0
68	100,000	678,549	1,154,250		100,000	570,931	0
69	0	718,051	1,192,261		0	590,057	0
70	0	759,576	1,231,438		0	609,824	0
71	100,000	697,709	1,104,861		100,000	526,903	0
72	0	737,802	1,141,702		0	544,555	0
73	0	779,925	1,180,221		0	562,797	0
74	0	824,217	1,220,447		0	581,651	0
75	75,000	793,085	1,180,389		75,000	523,522	0
76	0	839,156	1,220,126		0	540,956	0
77	0	887,371	1,270,693		0	558,970	0
78	0	937,769	1,310,211		0	577,583	0
79	0	990,352	1,359,908		0	596,817	0
80	$0	$1,045,110	$1,379,254		$0	616,691	$0

On the left hand side of the chart, you see where you take out $100,000 a year (which is what your $150,000 in the investment account netted after taxes) at ages 66, 67, and 70, and $75,000 at age 75. At the end of 15 years, you have a remaining cash value of $1,045,110, plus a death benefit of $1,379,524, which will continue to grow. Between the $2,000,000 that you invested in the chart above, where you took at $150,000 (which got reduced by taxes to $100,000) in most years, and the whole life insurance, where you took out $100,000 (tax free) in the short years, you got to preserve and grow the $2,000,000, plus have cash value life insurance, and a death benefit.

Summary: If you had taken out $150,000 every year from the $2,000,000 investment in this example, at the end of 15 years, you would have $1,001,147. If you instead switched between the investment account and the whole life insurance policy, you would have $3,356,013 in the investment account, plus $1,045,110 in cash value, plus a death benefit! And the cash value and death benefit will keep on growing.

What's missing from this discussion? Obviously, if you had not been paying life insurance premiums from ages 45 through 65, you would have had $26,470 a year to spend or invest in something else.

So let's revise the scenario. Assume that at age 45, you had taken out a $1,000,000 term life insurance policy for 20 years, instead of whole life. Your annual premium cost would have been $1,885 (approximately), leaving $24,585 a year to invest (the difference between the term premium and the whole life premium). Assume you put this in an account that earned 5% a year, and that your taxes were 33.33% of the gain. This would have grown to $713,542 by age 65. Now, roll this over to a new investment at the same rate, and remove $100,000 at ages 66, 67, and 70, and $75,000 at age 75. You end up with $616,691 in 15 years, as shown on the right side of the chart above.

So at age 65, you have less cash, and no death benefit. By age 80, when you've removed money at ages 66, 67, 70, and 75, you are still farther behind than where you would have been had you bought whole life, and still, you have no death benefit.

In other words, even factoring in the different in the cost of insurance between term and whole life, you end up in a much better position at age 65, when you structure your retirement years' investments, and at age 80, when you are half way through your retirement.

I know this is complex, and confusing. We are talking several strategies at once—whole life insurance, taxable investment accounts, and annuities. And the returns we show are just one example. The point is not to recommend any particular combination, or predict what will happen. What I am trying to show is that you have many options, and that if you are clever about how you structure your investments, and understand how rates of return really work, you can make your money work harder and last longer. You can plan smart, and do well—I just can't quantify how *much* better you can do. The key is making sure that you have both defensive and offensive investments, so you do not have to take money out of any particular investment at the wrong time.

A final word about annuities, since I mentioned putting money in either an annuity or an investment account: Annuities are complex, and they have a lot of bell and whistles, and can be structured differently to meet different needs. In order to understand annuities, you will have to become comfortable with the following terms:

- GMIB—Guaranteed Minimum Income Benefit—an option that you can purchase that will guarantee you at least a minimum return on your investment
- GMWB—Guaranteed Minimum Withdrawal Benefit—an option you can purchase that will allow you to withdraw money every year, until you initial premium has been returned to you, irrespective of market performance
- GMAB—Guaranteed Minimum Accumulation Benefit—protects the amount on which you can draw income on from market variations
- GLWB—Guaranteed Lifetime Withdrawal Benefit—an option you can purchase that allows you to withdraw a certain amount for your lifetime, irrespective of account value.
- EBD—Enhanced Death Benefit—an option you can purchase that insures that a certain sum will go to your heirs when you die.

As you can see, there are a lot of options, and each comes with a cost. Make sure you and your advisor pick the ones most appropriate for your financial situation.

Annuities are also useful vehicles for passing money to your heirs while reducing taxes that need to be paid. I'm not going to get into details here—wealth transfer is a huge and technical subject—but you may want to Google explanations of GRAT (Grantor Retained Annuity Trusts), QTIP (Qualified Terminable Interest Property, GST (Generation Skipping Trust),QRPT (Qualified Personal Residence Trust), FLP (Family Limited Partnership), CRT (Charitable Remainder Trust), and other related terms. They all need not involve annuities, but annuities are a common way to generate income for one generation while leaving assets to another, or to a charity, while providing income to you.

"*Everything you need to know about our finances is in this stack here, unless, of course, it's somewhere else.*"

LIST 10: I'M RETIRED, NOW WHAT?

Technically, this isn't a list. This section is an admonition, and a message of encouragement.

First, the admonition:

Retirement is a perilous time financially, because, by definition, earned income has stopped coming in, and your ability to act and think independently has started to diminish.

I know you resent the last part of that statement, and you think it doesn't apply to you. Well, maybe not now. But it will, eventually, and it will probably creep up on you. So start planning now to have someone a generation younger, who you trust absolutely (a child, your children as a group, an advisor, a professional) be part of all your financial decisions, so they know what is where, and how to access assets. Involve them in making major decisions, even just as a sounding board. It doesn't mean that you are incompetent (even though some states, notably Florida, assume that the minute you turn 65, you become an idiot. Others, like Pennsylvania, assume that you are an idiot the minute you turn 18.) Remember, because you are retired, your chances to recover from bad decisions are limited. A client of mine, who is getting near retirement, sums it up well: "Fear, not greed." You need safety, and reassurance that you will have enough money to live on, no matter what. Now is not the time to be ambitious or aggressive. At this stage of your life, your financial decisions need to be conservative.

You need to make a list of what your expenses will be, in sickness and in health. Then, you need to figure out how you are going to meet these expenses.

Next, the words of encouragement:

There are a lot of options open to you. Annuities are wonderful income management and guarantee instruments. If your health is good, you are not too old for permanent life insurance. You are certainly not too old to take out long term care insurance. The key is to budget carefully. And make sure your money is invested in safe assets, where principal is guaranteed.

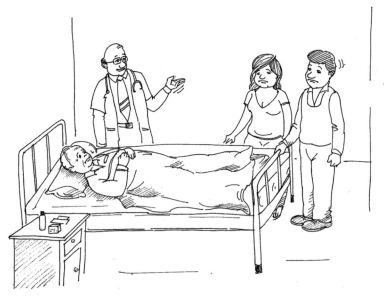

"I can't pull the plug to end his suffering—he's not plugged in to anything.

LIST 11: THREE FACTS YOU NEED TO KNOW ABOUT THE COST OF AGING (LONG TERM CARE)

FACT #1: Aging poorly will cost more than you think.

What happens if you are disabled, or become disabled, or need some sort of extra care, after retirement age, (when you no longer have disability insurance coverage)?

Who pays for the care you need once medical insurance coverage no longer applies? (For instance, when 90 days pass after a hospitalization and your condition stabilizes, but you are still not able to care for yourself, and you are not getting better?)

Who pays for care if you just gradually age, without any traumatic event, but just become increasingly fragile, or unable to take care of yourself? (Such as not feeding and dressing yourself, or getting out of bed unassisted?)

Who pays for care if you become increasingly disoriented, and your children realize that it is no longer safe for you to be left alone?

If you've planned properly, you already have retirement income coming in. This may be income from investments, retirement plans, pensions, and social security—any source of income that does not come from having to go to work. If you planned properly, you calculated what would be sufficient to support your anticipated retirement lifestyle. But most people do not factor in ill health, disability, or the ravages of old age into these expense calculations. All the advertisements you see for retirement funds show elegant, upscale and physically fit retirees. They are dining by moonlight, or at a clubhouse, or walking leisurely on the beach, or playing shuffleboard or tennis, or visiting museums, or taking cruises. I have yet to see a retirement ad showing an otherwise healthy person in rehab after hip replacement or a fall, or being wheeled through a supermarket by a caretaker. The ads never show a retiree getting off a wheelchair-carrying van to visit yet another doctor. But the fact is, even if you are still healthy and fully functional when you reach age 65, chances are about 66% for women and over 40% for men, that you will need some sort of long term care for more than 90 days before you die. And there will be expenses associated with that care that are not part of your "healthy lifestyle" retirement budget.

Aging poorly is a disability, just as an accident or illness is at a younger age.

But unlike your working years, when disability and health insurance will replace lost income and help with some additional expenses, disability in retirement is **NOT** funded by anything other than long term care insurance, or some other source of income above and beyond what you budgeted for a healthy retirement.

Medicare and health insurance will **NOT** pay for long term care.

If you have no means to pay for long term care, you and your spouse's standard of living may suffer.

The quality of your life in your last years will be determined not so much by your health, but by how you planned to pay for your care if you are in poor health. The government chips in only when you become impoverished. Do you want poverty, and the government, dictating your care in your most frail years?

FACT # 2: You can plan now to pay for the cost of aging when you need it.

You will probably live longer than your parents, but not as well, in terms of health. It is not as obvious as it sounds. We conquered many of the major diseases that killed people young in the "old days." Look back at the biographies of your relatives who died before 1950—chances are that people who are dying today, at the same age that your relatives were, are not dying of the same diseases. In fact, chances are today that they are still alive at the age your grandparents and great-grandparents died. Today, if you live beyond your sixties, you have a good chance of living for a long while—most of the killer diseases that were killing people at the beginning of the last century are not going to kill you. Plus, you've already discovered the chronic conditions that will be with you for the rest of your life, and you've learned to manage these conditions! They are "under control," in the sense that you are actively doing something about them—you are treating them, doing therapy, watching your diet, immunizing yourself, etc. The disease that you are being treated for may not be what is going to kill you. It is increasingly likely that the disease you are aware of will be managed, and that it will be something that was <u>not</u> diagnosed that proves fatal. The successful management of the diagnosed disease may keep you alive until old age kicks in, when something else fails. For example, my Dad had chronic low level leukemia for 30 years. It was being managed. What killed him was his heart. The heart condition was undiagnosed until 5 months before he died, at which point it was too late to do anything.

But it is not just that we are living longer; the life we live, when we do live longer, is a lot different than it was in the "old days." Because the ill people in the old days tended to die younger, the older folks back then were <u>healthier</u> than they are today. Having survived until old age, they were strong, and many of them tended to go suddenly, or after a short illness. There was less "lingering," for lack of a better term. By lingering, I mean the slow deterioration of multiple body parts and functions—the slow descent into being less and less active, less and less cognizant of the surroundings, less and less mobile. Someone reaching retirement age today stands a better chance than ever of making it to "old age." But they are also more likely to deteriorate away, and not die suddenly. The new "old age" is different than what old age looked like when you were a kid.

What does this mean for you?

It means that you need to have a plan in place to fund the disabilities of old age.

Medicare does not provide long-term care. Your resources in old age are going to be whatever Social Security provides, the assets you've accumulated, pensions and retirement funds (if you have any, and if they survive corporate upheavals), and insurance and annuities. If you've budgeted only for your living expenses with these, you still have not provided for the supplemental income you will need when you incur the additional expenses associated with being less able to care for yourself. Relying on a spouse who is also aging, or on children who are raising children of their own, may not be a failsafe option. Long-term care insurance is specifically designed to meet these additional expenses and needs.

The next question is: Where are you going to live in your old age? The choices are:

- In your home.
- In your child's/relative's home.

- In a retirement facility (either a group setting, or an individual apartment with communal dining).
- In an assisted living facility.
- In a skilled nursing facility.
- In a nursing home.

Let's look at what these choices mean:
- Your home or a child/relative's home. Who is going to provide the care? Are family members going to be the primary caregivers, or will you need to hire outside help? Even if you assume that housing costs will be minimal, the expense of live-in or part-time help can be considerable, and it is not covered by Medicare. And even with the best of relative caregivers, you need to factor in costs for respite care—your caregivers are going to need some time off. Don't make the mistake of relying on a spouse—if he or she is close to your age, he or she may not be up to the task. Or may need care him or herself.
- A facility—this adds housing costs to the mix, and does not always remove the cost of private care. Even in the best of facilities, many patients have private duty care to supplement one-on-one the services provided by the staff. This individual attention, even if provided just during waking hours, can run tens of thousands of dollars a year extra. But it provides a higher level of care, and may result in better outcomes for the patient.

In a nutshell:
The less you can do for yourself, the more help you will need, and the more it will cost. The older you get, the greater the likelihood that your care needs will increase. The government will not provide this care unless you become

impoverished, and are eligible for Medicaid. If you want to hold onto your assets, or if you want to have sufficient funds to provide the type of care you would like to have, you should consider long-term care insurance.

FACT # 3: There are several options for long term care.

Option One: "Traditional" Long-Term Care Insurance (LTCI)

Although sometimes thought of as a new product, long-term care insurance has been around for several decades in various forms. It is only recently that there have been significant advancements in this type of insurance product, providing more versatility, and making it better suited to real life needs and conditions.

Since insurance companies are constantly coming out with new long-term care products, it is appropriate to re-visit older policies that you may have to see if they are still the best fit for your needs. Also, over time, your needs may have changed, so the policy your bought years ago may not adequately cover your current projected needs For instance, one client who I spoke to about LTC insurance assured me that she did not need a policy—her mother had taken one out for her over a decade ago, so she was covered. When we looked at the policy (which had a very low annual premium that the mother continued to pay), we discovered that is would pay for care for up to two years, at a maximum of $50 a day, only in a facility run by Christian Scientists. (I am not making this up—many people bought these types of polices.) Since today's needs are about $150 a day, and an average of four years of care are needed between the onset of symptoms requiring care and death, this was clearly inadequate. Plus, we could not find any facilities nearby run by Christian Scientists.

Even if we could, this client subscribed to a different religion, which was incompatible with Christian Science.

Similarly, many people have polices as part of their employment, at low or no cost to them. But even a cursory look at these policies show that the length of covered care and the maximum allowed reimbursement is wholly inadequate.

Another phenomenon in the marketplace is that insurance companies are leaving the long term care market, as costs exceed expenses, making many older policies unprofitable. One side effect of this has been increases in premiums for many customers, which come as a surprise to most, since they thought (erroneously) that premiums were fixed for life.

Before we look at the details of long-term care insurance, and how today's policies differ from older policies, I want to address what these changes mean to people who have previously purchased long-term care insurance, and who have older policies in force. But first, I need to strongly emphasize several key factors pertaining to existing policies, for those who have them. If this is repetitive, I apologize, but I'd rather overstate than understate these key points:

* **DO NOT give up an existing policy unless you are ABSOLUTELY SURE you do not want it**—you will not be able to replace it once you surrender it. If anyone advises you to cancel an existing policy, get a second opinion before you walk away from it. Let me repeat this to be absolutely clear. **DO NOT GIVE UP EXISTING LONG-TERM CARE INSURANCE POLICIES UNTIL YOU ARE ABSOLUTELY SURE THAT YOU DO NOT WANT THEM ANYMORE— YOU CANNOT REINSTATE THEM LATER.**
* The age of an existing policy does not automatically mean that it is either appropriate or inappropriate

for you. A lot depends on the particular policy, your current and projected circumstances, and what other resources you have available.

❖ If you feel that you do not have enough coverage, sometimes it is advisable to supplement an existing policy with a newer policy offering additional features and benefits. Having two policies can be an appropriate way to balance the savings on premium in an older policy with the enhanced benefits of a new, additional policy.

❖ Because you were (much) younger when you bought your current policy, your premiums are generally (much) lower than you would pay today. Even if the coverage is not ideal, the benefits provided by an existing policy may be worth retaining. It might not be the type of policy you would buy today as a starter policy, but even if some of the coverage seems unnecessary or insufficient, it may make sense in terms of total premium outlay.

It is generally desirable to keep existing policies. Be very cautious before abandoning a policy that you have paid premiums into for a while. Make sure that it is abundantly clear that you are better off starting anew before you cancel existing policies.

However, if you find your existing policy lacking in coverage, you may want to consider adding a supplemental policy to cover the gaps, while keeping what you already have.

Here's how I like to think of long-term care insurance:

o I may live out my life, vigorous to the end, not needing help, and dying suddenly. If this happens, and I hope it does, I will not have collected any financial benefits from my LTC insurance—just peace of mind. (Unless I have a hybrid policy—see below. It will buy me long-term care protection, plus pay back more than I spent if I don't need long-term care.)

o In the more likely case that I will deteriorate at some point in time, my LTC policy will provide supplemental income to take care of the increased expenses I incur. Depending on the type of policy I buy, I will either:

- be reimbursed for out of pocket expenses up to a preset limit (reimbursement policy), or
- be paid a set amount for every day I receive care (daily indemnity benefit), or
- I will receive a flat monthly check, to spend as I wish, irrespective of my expenses (monthly indemnity policy or rider).

In all three cases, the insurance is designed to pay for the care necessary to leave the rest of my environment (my financial situation, and my ability to receive the care I need with minimal upset to me and my family) intact. To me, long-term care insurance is just disability insurance for old age—it is income replacement or supplement income for the disability of aging past 65.

Things to look for in an LTC policy:

▪ **Home care, community care, facility care**—some policies only cover some of these. If you want the option of receiving care without going into an institution, make sure your policy provides for this.
▪ **Monthly benefit rider**—pays 31x the daily rate for home care, up to actual cost, instead of requiring you to have care daily, and submit receipts covering each day.

- **Shortened benefit nonforfeiture**—after you pay premiums for a certain length of time, generally three years, you still get some benefits if the policy lapses— usually up to the amount you paid in premiums.
- **Elimination period**—a number of days that need to elapse between the time you qualify and the time benefits start—usually 90 days. Some riders speed up the elimination period, like counting one day of care a week as if you were receiving care every day.
- **Waiver of elimination period**—sets elimination period to zero days in some circumstances, usually home based care.
- **Covered partner waiver of premium**—if you start to receive benefits, your partner no longer has to pay premiums to keep his or her policy in force.
- **Paid up survivor benefit**—after a certain period of time, usually 10 years, you no longer have to pay your premium if your partner dies.
- **Inflation protection**—guaranteed annual increase in benefits, selected at time of initial contract. This is expensive, but important. If your benefits remain stagnant, the amount of daily coverage you purchase today may not be adequate for the costs decades from now.
- **Total lifetime benefits**—choose either a certain amount per day, with a total lifetime cap, of unlimited lifetime benefits. If you choose, for example, $300 a day with a five year benefit period, the total lifetime benefit is $300 x 365 x 5, or $547,500. If you do not have lifetime coverage, and you want to extend the benefits for a longer period of time, you would have to take less than $300 a day. To make calculations easy, let's say you just took half of the maximum–$150 daily—then you would have coverage for ten years,

or twice as long. But you don't need to buy lifetime coverage—it can be overkill. Most people use three to five years of benefits before they die, so if you fund six or eight years, you should have more than enough coverage, and your costs will be lower. However, these are just averages. My mother-in-law was in a nursing home for 27 years!

- **Partnership policies**—Several states offer partnership policies, which protect your assets if your LTC insurance run out, by providing you with Medicaid funds. Normally, in order to qualify for Medicaid, you have to be impoverished—with $2,000 or less in assets. Once you reach this level, Medicaid pitches in and pays for some long term care costs. The good news is that you are getting long term care; the bad news is that you are destitute (and, yes, they check carefully for make sure you haven't given away all your money in the past five years, hidden assets, or gave everything you own to your kids.) To encourage people to take out long term care insurance, partnership programs were created. They work as follows: if you take out a long term care policy that meets certain minimum requirements (like built-in inflation protection), worth, say, $500,000 in benefits, and you need long term care, and you use up all $500,000, then Medicaid will kick in when the value of your assets equals the poverty level ($2,000) plus $500,000. If you have a million dollars in benefits, then Medicaid kicks in while you still have a million dollars in assets. Essentially, the partnership program lets you keep substantial assets to pass on to your heirs, to the extent you've provided for long term care. Your insurance agent can tell you what policies qualify for partnership protection at no additional cost to you. They vary by your age and the state you reside in.

- **Dividends**—No insurance company can promise you that premiums will not go up for long term care insurance. By law, they are allowed to raise rates for all individuals covered by a particular type of policy if they can prove actuarially that they need higher premiums to pay anticipated claims. (See below.) But if you have a dividend paying policy, the first place they will go for more money is to the dividends, before they seek to raise rates.

What are your chances for needing long-term care? The numbers keep changing, and it is greater for single people than married people, but something like 66% of women (40% of men) who live to age 65 will need some long term care later on in life. Once you start receiving long term care benefits, chances that you will need it for more than 3 years is about 15% (and 5% for more than five years). At current rates, depending on where you live, between $150 and $200 a day funds basic care.

One word of caution about long term care policies. Most policies obligate you to pay premiums for your lifetime, or until you start drawing benefits. While premiums are calculated so that they remain level from year to year, the companies have the right to raise premiums for everyone (not you alone) if they find that costs are exceeding revenues. And that is exactly what happened in the past few years—as more and more people took out long term care polices, and some started collecting benefits, the insurance companies discovered that older policies were underpriced. So they went back and raised the annual rates, often substantially. This is bad news for people on fixed incomes. The policy holder's only recourse was to pay the higher rates, accept reduce benefits, or get back benefits equal to the premiums they paid in. While the insurance companies have revised their prices for new policies higher, there is no assurance repricing won't happen again, either on older or newer policies. The only way to avoid a price increase is to buy a policy with a limited pay-in period, like a 10 year pay, or a pay until age 65 policy, and hope the rates won't go up before the ten years are up, or you reach age 65.

Option Two: "Double Duty" Insurance

What if you end up never needing long-term care?

Good for you! Even though you are more likely than not to eventually qualify to receive long-term care benefits, there still is a good chance that you may not. In that case, you would not have received a financial benefit from the LTC premiums you paid. (I am not counting the peace of mind of knowing you had the protection.) However, if you had elected to purchase a "shared benefits" rider, the funds you did not use would be available to your spouse while you are alive, should his or her benefits run out. This is a relatively inexpensive rider that can effectively double coverage.

But there is another option that guarantees a financial return on your premiums. More and more companies are introducing a hybrid permanent insurance, which builds cash value and has a death benefit, which lets you collect on most of the death benefit BEFORE you die, if you qualify for long-term care. The premiums for this insurance are going to be higher than LTC premiums, but over time you may build cash value, and you are guaranteed a pay out when you die. Of course, the death benefit is reduced by the amount you took prior to death, and the coverage for LTC may not be as high, or for as long a period, as a straight LTC policy. A word of caution: Examine the provisions of these policies carefully. Sometimes the advertised benefits are greater than the actual benefits. At least one company promises that you can access 24% of your death benefit a year for long term care. So if you have a $500,000 death benefit, you would think that you could get $120,000 a year for long term care. In actuality, the amount they would actually pay is lower—it depends on your age when you access this benefit. This type of policy is designed for people who expect to need long term care towards the end of their life, when they are old, and has less money available if it turns out that you need it in middle age or early in retirement. Nevertheless, it is a financially sound investment—you always get a death benefit, and even if you live to be over 100, the return on your premium is decent.

Option Three: Other Resources

A third option is a high cash value policy, which involves a substantial, one time initial premium. If you use it for long-term care, it will more than triple in value. If you don't use it, it will have a death benefit greater than the premium paid. And if you decide you want your money back at any time, you can surrender the policy and get 100% of your premium back. Your only cost is the loss of use over time of the money you paid. (These policies have a lot of variations, and allow for a lot of alternatives, such as using part for long-term care, and leaving a smaller death benefit—we can go over details if this appeals to you.) Buying a policy like this is like having a 20 year, or more, "free look" provision—you can decide at any time that you don't want it, and get your money back. The only cost is what your money would have earned for you in another investment over that period of time.

Also, you can use traditional whole life, which builds cash value over time, to help pay for long term care. After a decade or two, cash value really starts to build in these policies, so if you need to take out a policy loan later on, there are funds available. Of course, the amount available depends on the size of the policy, and you have to be careful to not withdraw so much money that the policy lapses.

Option Four: Bad Ideas

Some people opt for bad choices.

The primary bad choice I hear is: "My spouse will take care of me." This sounds like it is well-intentioned, but unless you are married to someone a generation younger than you, chances are that neither of you will be in a position to take good care of each other. Which means it will fall on your children, which is not a good idea for three reasons:

- They may not be able to take care of you—their life circumstances may not allow it. Chances are they will have enough trouble caring for their own children, and planning their own retirement.
- They may not want to take care of you, no matter how well you raised them. Or their spouse may not want to take care of you.
- It could ruins both your lives. It may disrupt their lives thoroughly, and lead to divorce, job loss, or worse, and you may not get the level of care you need.

And if a family member (spouse or child) does take care of you, you have to remember that it will take a toll on them. Chances are that they did not plan on spending years of their life this way, and they are probably ill-equipped to staff all three shifts that caring for an invalid requires.

There was an article in the newspaper recently (I am not making this up) about a man who was arrested for housing his elderly mother in a shed in his garden. When the authorities found her, she was dehydrated, and on the verge of death. She had been living in a room inside the house, but when he lost his job, he moved her out to make room for a rent-paying tenant.

Elder abuse is a problem. It was a huge problem when I moved to Florida in 1975, and I was part of a group that investigated elder abuse in homes and institutions, and brought about major reforms and regulations. Now it's 2011, and I'm still reading stories about abuses by institutions and individuals. And stories about legislators who are shocked, and promising to pass more laws. And 36 years from now, my children will be reading contemporary versions of the same stories. I won't. I'll be in a very pleasant retirement home that my long term care insurance policy will be paying for.

"Never bought disability insurance—after all, what's the real chance of something happening to me?"

LIST 12: PAYCHECK INSURANCE (KEEPING YOUR PAYCHECK COMING WHEN YOU CAN'T GO TO WORK)

What would happen if you didn't have a paycheck one week? What would happen if this went on for several weeks in a row? What would happen if this went on indefinitely, for a few years, or more? It's a horrible thought to contemplate—your life, as you know it now, would change dramatically, and not for the better.

There are two types of people in the world: the physically fully functioning (the "abled"), and the disabled. You are one or the other (although the extent of your disability can vary). And you usually go from being abled to disabled VERY quickly—in seconds (in an accident), in minutes (in a disaster or natural catastrophe, or a sudden stroke or heart attack), or in days or weeks (with degenerative illnesses). Sometimes, the march toward disability is slow, like when arthritis or tremors slowly makes it harder to perform the tasks you do while working, until, one day, you just have to stop. But that is rare, as is total disability. Most of the time, the transition is from "abled" to "partly disabled," and it happens quickly.

Disability has nothing to do with the type of work you do. Sure, some jobs are more dangerous than others, but most disabling events happen outside of work, or due to accident, illness, or disease.

And when disabling events happen, most often, your income is impacted immediately. The paychecks stop coming right away.

For most people, missing just one paycheck is a problem. Missing two or three paychecks is a disaster. For most people, there are limited savings, and they get eaten up quickly when there is no paycheck. Sometimes, savings are not liquid—they can be invested in a house, or a retirement fund. Cashing out may mean losing money, or losing your home. It can mean losing your retirement nest egg. Any many people are getting by, one paycheck to the next. Their expenses are too great to begin savings. And the thought of unemployment, due to disability or anything else, is too traumatic to even contemplate.

So why, when you can spend 2% or 3% of your paycheck and get paycheck insurance (also known as disability insurance), don't more people have it? Your paycheck is your most valuable asset. The younger you are, the more it is worth. Year after year, your paycheck can add up to millions of dollars, or more. If you lose it, all your plans for the future are drastically altered.

I don't understand why people hide from this fact. It makes no sense. When I ask people about disability insurance, and they refuse to discuss it, my attitude is: "Okay, so let's just write a letter to your spouse, or child, and put it in an envelope that is marked "To be opened in the event I am incapacitated." Now, write what you want your child or spouse to read while you are in a coma, in the hospital. Start by saying—"Honey, I know you are glad that I am still alive after what I just went through. Unfortunately, we're poor now, because my paycheck will stop coming in next week. I never bothered to buy disability insurance because I never thought this would happen, and because…" and then fill in an excuse." I tried this once. My anger got the best of me, because they guy was making several hundred thousand dollars a year, and his wife took care of the four children, who were in private school. Needless to say, the guy kicked me out of his office, and won't return my calls. But I have a feeling he wasn't going to listen to anything I had to say about his financial future. And get this—he's a lawyer, he advises clients to buy disability insurance, and one of his clients was sitting in a car at a stop light, right in front of his office, just four months prior, was badly injured, and he handled the lawsuit!

There are no good numbers on the percentage of working people who are disabled for 90 days or more in their careers, but the number is high—higher than:

- the percentage of people who total their cars once in their lifetimes
- the percentage of people who have a major fire, theft, or other loss to their home once in their lifetimes
- the percentage of people who are under 65 now and who will die in the next 20 years.

Yet most people have:

- Car insurance
- Homeowners or renters insurance
- and some sort of term life insurance (either on their own or through work).

In other words, most of us have insurance on things that are less likely to happen, than on something we know is much more likely to occur. We are better insured to handle losses that are not likely to occur than we are to cover the losses from a more common disaster, which would have devastating consequences. Loss of a paycheck for more than a few months would reduce most people to welfare status. It could cost us millions of dollars in our lifetime.

(Note: Social Security provides disability benefits for working people. But they are limited, and hard to get. It takes time, there are denials of coverage, and in many cases, the disability is deemed as not being eligible. And the amount received is generally less than your paycheck.)

So unless you are independently wealthy, and don't need a paycheck, you want to have some disability insurance.

Here's what to look for when researching a policy, and comparing plans:

Guaranteed premiums: Get a policy where premiums are guaranteed not to go up until age 65. (Most policies will not cover you beyond age 65 or 70).

Waiver of premium: If you are disabled, make sure no premiums are required after 90 days of disability, and you get back the premiums you paid in the previous 90 days.

No offset for Social Security: if you do collect Social Security disability payments, make sure your private policy does not cut back what it pays you.

Definition of disabled: Pay more for a policy that covers you if you cannot work in your own field (**own occupation**) if you are highly trained, and if you would return to work in a different occupation while you are partially disabled, and that work will pay significantly less than you are making now. For instance, if you are a trained surgeon, and would make less as a practicing physician who did not practice surgery, or if you are a trial lawyer, and you would make less if you were not able to go to court, then you want "own occupation" coverage. On the other hand, if you would be able to return to work and make similar money in a different field, while partially disabled, you may not want to spend money on an "own occupation" rider. It is more likely that you will be partially disabled than totally disabled, and more likely that you will be able to work at some job. If you end up being totally disabled, or presumptively totally disabled, then "own occupation" doesn't matter—you'll be getting full benefits. It is just if you are partially disabled that this provision would be important.

(I know this may not be clear—please discussed this with your insurance advisor before buying disability insurance—it is complex.)

Benefit period: get a policy that covers you as long as possible (until retirement), with at most a 90 day waiting period for benefits to begin. (Shorter waiting periods are very expensive, and not worth it; longer ones can be a burden if you do get disabled.)

Extended partial disability: Disability is not all or nothing—look for benefits that give you credit for partial disability. You are more likely to be partially disabled than totally disabled.

Cost of living: This rider is a must. It protects you against inflation.

Future insurability option: The right to increase your benefits **WITHOUT** having to qualify medically, based solely on an increase in your earned income.

Retirement plan contributions: Are you participating in a retirement plan, or will you in the future? Make sure you consider buying a rider that will continue those contributions if you are disabled.

Paying for disability insurance: If you pay the premium with after tax dollars, your benefits are not subject to income tax. If your employer pays with before tax dollars, your benefits are income taxable. Since most policies provide benefits equal to 60% of your salary, it makes sense to use after tax dollars to pay for disability insurance, since the disability check you receive will be close to your take home pay.

How are benefits computed? Make sure you understand this, and have your insurance agent show you where in the policy this is explained. Most likely, if you are totally disabled, you will receive the full amount of the benefit you signed up for, adjusted for cost of living (because you purchased a cost of living rider) and adjusted to your current income (because you purchased a future income rider, and you exercised it). Your income at the time of your disability will not be a factor. But if you are partially disabled, your income prior to becoming disabled will matter in determining your benefits.

How to buy paycheck insurance: You may have noticed that I mentioned, several times, speaking to your insurance agent. Disability insurance is something you want to buy from an agent in person, not through the mail, or on the Internet. It is too complex. Your agent should be able to work with you to get you the best possible coverage, at the best possible rate. Unlike life insurance, which is based on health and age, disability insurance also considers the type of work you do. And how you are classified affects your rates and benefits. Also, it gives you the opportunity to ask your agent about his or her disability insurance. If he or she does not have disability insurance, you may want to ask why he or she is recommending it to you?

A good website to checkout is www.protectyourpaycheck. org or www.lifehappens.org. It is hosted by LIFE, a non-profit organization funded by disability insurers, but it makes a good case for disability insurance, and has helpful details in calculating how much you need.

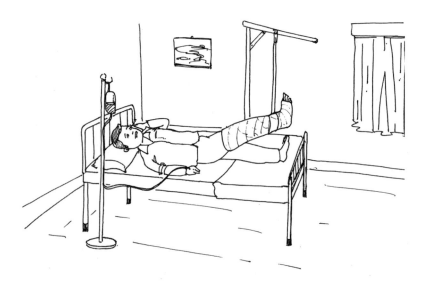

"I'm sure they'll keep paying my salary—I've done so much for the firm."

LIST 13: FAMILY BUSINESSES

Family businesses or other closely held businesses often represent a substantial portion of an individual's assets. It is extremely important to have a plan in place that covers:

- Retirement
- Turning over the business to heirs
- Turning over the business to successors while you are alive
- Continuing the business if you are disabled

In each case, you need to have thought through and funded mechanisms to either buy you out, or provide you with income, in the event you are no longer working. It is especially important to have made arrangements for financial liquidity, to either pay taxes (in the event of inheritance) or to buy you out, or to continue your compensation in the event you are no longer able to work (due to disability). You also need to provide for a way for family members who are not going to continue in the business to be able to access the value of their ownership.

Let's consider four areas of concern separately:

Death:

- How is the business going to be capitalized to minimize estate taxes?
- How will the estate pay the taxes due if ownership changes in whole or in part due to death?

- How will non-involved family members be compensated when ownership changes?
- How will sufficient cash flow be provided to fund the business, pay creditors, or provide indemnification until the key person can be replaced?

Disability:

- What salary continuation plan is in effect, and how will it be funded?
- With what funds will the disabled key employee's replacement be paid?

Retirement:

- What deferred compensation plans need to be created to provide a tax effective plan?
- What incentives need to be put in place for key people to stay on?

Transfer of Ownership:

- What does the buy-sell agreement look like?
- What are the details—purchaser, price, method of payment?
- What will prompt a sale (death, retirement, disability)?
- How will proceeds be invested?

The point of raising all these questions is not to try to resolve them in such a short space. Rather, by identifying these issues, we are hoping to make it clear that where a family or closely held business is involved, these types of questions need to be addressed before there is an immediate need to answer them, especially if insurance is going to be a vehicle to fund the solutions. Also, each business, and each family will be different—no shorthand list is going to adequately address all the aspects of each situation.

In addition to determining the financial ramifications of the above scenarios, you have to make sure the assets of the business are properly titled for the plans you put in place. Often, the tax consequences of an event triggering a financial change are determined not only by what happens, but how the underlying assets are owned and titled.

If your financial situation includes a closely held or family business, you need to address the particulars of your situation both with an attorney and a financial consultant to make sure all the issues are covered.

"Unfortunately, your late father did not leave a will or life insurance, so we'll sell everything else to pay debts, taxes and probate attorney fees. But you may each take one memento."

LIST 14: I'M WEALTHY, NOW WHAT?

You don't have to have a family business, or an inheritance, to be wealthy. It is possible to be employed, or have made good investments, or just have been cautious about spending, and you may end up with more money than you can spend in your lifetime, and then some.

If that is the case, first of all, congratulations!

Whether your wealth is sudden, or has gradually accumulated, you need to protect this wealth, so that it does not dissipate when you die, or get taken from you through adverse proceedings.

Let's deal with death first. There are two bad things can happen when a wealthy person dies:

- Estate taxes. The government levies a tax if your estate is large enough. The tax needs to be paid quickly, and if your estate does not have enough liquid assets, like cash and easily convertible monetary instruments, your heirs may have to liquidate some assets at unfavorable rates to raise the necessary cash. Chances are, if you've been enjoying your wealth, and not merely hoarding it, you own things like art, real estate, collections, and the like, and you may have to take a loss if you sell suddenly. Or your wealth may be invested in businesses, which are not easy to sell quickly at a good price. There are countless examples of people who did not plan properly for estate taxes, and the fortune they thought they were leaving to their heirs was substantially reduced, or disappeared, as a result.

A notable recent example is Joe Robbie, who died in 1990. Joe owned the winning NFL football team, the Miami Dolphins, during its heyday, and also the Joe Robbie Stadium, where they played home games. His family lost both because they had to sell to pay estate taxes, and the money that was supposed to provide them happiness left bitterness instead. It could have been avoided. Another example is Jacqueline Kennedy Onassis, who had wanted to leave her estate to charity and her family. Due to poor planning, less than half a million dollars ended up going to charity, and the bulk went to pay taxes.

- Unforeseen circumstances—Children who inherit wealth may not know how to handle it, or may not put adequate protection in place to safeguard it. Assets passed on to children without restrictions can go to pay judgments, be squandered, or lost in divorce proceedings. If the life circumstances of the person who dies changed before their death (divorce, loss of spouse, loss of a child, adoption, etc.), the prior estate plans may not be current, and that can mean that money will be lost to taxes, or given to someone you'd rather not have it.

Aside from death, wealth is threatened by the litigious nature of our society. If you have money, and someone can prove that you are at fault for causing someone else harm, chances are that some lawyer will see an opportunity to sue, to take your money away from you. Even if you think that you are not at fault, you are still liable to being sued. And if you have wealth, or any unprotected assets, they are at risk, unless you protect them.

For instance, I was sued for $300,000 by a classmate of one of my children, who broke her ankle while roller skating with him during a youth group outing. She wasn't claiming that he pushed her, or acted maliciously—she just claimed that he touched her while they were skating. He admits it–skating while holding hands, or in a line, with one person's hands on another's hips, is a commonly enjoyed activity among skaters. And inexperienced skaters are apt to fall. The ankle mended nicely, in a cast for four weeks, and, as is usual with childhood broken bones, there is no lasting damage.

That was three years ago. The lawsuit is dragging on. The reason I was sued was because I have $300,000, and the father (an attorney) saw an opportunity. Fortunately, I have homeowner's insurance and umbrella insurance, so my out of pocket costs will be minimal, whatever the outcome. The insurance company bears the burden of the defense, and paying whatever judgment emerges. I was outraged at the whole action and process, and urged them to fight the case. After all, this was accidental, and breaking a leg is a known risk that occasional skaters take on when they put on unfamiliar skates and attempt to glide around the rink. Falling is normal; injuries happen; she recovered.

The insurance company estimates that the case is "worth" $90,000—that is what they think a reasonable settlement is! This does not include legal fees. The father offered to settle for $250,000. We're going to court.

The point of the story is not how ridiculous and disgusting this whole process is, nor the damage the process does to two children who were friends and are now being forced to testify against each other under oath, in a court, nor what is does to the social relationships in the youth group. These are all important points, but deserve a story of their own. My point here is that if you had asked me to list all the financial risks and hazards I thought my family and I would ever be exposed to, in my entire life, I do not know that this would appear anywhere on the list, ever. It just would not have crossed my mind. Yet had I not had proper insurance, I could have been out of pocket between $90,000 and $250,000, plus attorney fees. Ouch! I would have been forced to sell assets to cover the costs.

The reason I am including this story is to say, on a very personal level, that even though you may not think you are wealthy (I think I'm middle class), someone else might, and unless assets are properly titled, and insurance is in place, you can easily and unexpectedly lose what assets you've accumulated.

It does not have to end that way. Wealth can be preserved. Whether it is a lawsuit or estate taxes, or unexpected high medical or long term care costs, insurance can help you keep the money you've accumulated. Life insurance can be obtained to pay estate taxes (although planning precisely is difficult—the estate tax laws keep changing). And these protections can be extended to your heirs, for more than one generation.

Trusts can be set up to control the use of inherited funds. I won't go into specifics here, in part because the entire field of estate planning is complex, and estate lawyers are best equipped to deal with it. But just to give you an idea of the possibilities, here are some possible trusts that can be used:

- Charitable lead annuity trust (CLAT)—income goes to charity for a while, the remainder to heirs on favorable tax terms
- Credit shelter trust—maximizes estate tax exemption under rules in effect prior to 2010.
- Dynasty trust—some states allow these to transfer estate tax-free to subsequent generations.
- Grantor retained annuity trust (GRAT)—principal gets return to grantor with favorable tax treatment.
- Grantor trust—donors pay taxes on investment on behalf of heirs to avoid estate taxes.
- Qualified personal residence trust—transfer home ownership with favorable tax results.

- Qualified terminal interest property trust (QTIP)—can be used to provide children of a prior marriage with an estate, while providing income to a current spouse.
- Intentionally defective grantor trust sale—complex, and not completely safe way to transfer assets free of estate taxes
- Spousal access trust—irrevocable gift. Make sure you intend to stay married to the same person forever, and that the trustee you appoint will follow your wishes.
- Self-settled trusts—some people do it in some locations, even though these setups have not been thoroughly tested in court.

There are also gimmicks you can play with IRA's and Roth IRA's to get around limits on deferring taxes. Because the tax laws are so complex and change so frequently, unintended loopholes always crop up, and enterprising investors can often take advantage of them before they are changed.

You will also discover, at some point in time, that money may accumulate more rapidly than it did before. If you start saving while you are young, the effects of compounding interest or earnings can be dramatic. Even if you start saving in middle age, you still have 40 or 50 years of money growth ahead of you.

Remember the earlier example of the cup of coffee a day? In the first ten years of saving $3.33 a day, the accumulation was modest. In the next ten years, it started to rise noticeably. In the third decade, the rate of increase was dramatic, and in years thirty-one to forty, on a graph, it looked liked the value was shooting straight up. So if you do not have wealth now, and you plan on sticking around for a while, you may end up wealthy, and it would be a shame to lose it due to poor planning.

…and to my nephew Jim, who I promised to remember in my will, say "Hi Jim. I remember you."

LIST 15: FOUR DOCUMENTS YOU HAVE TO HAVE

You need to have a will, a durable power of attorney, a living will, and a document naming a health care surrogate.

DOCUMENT #1: Will

Everyone has an estate plan. But some people do not know what theirs is. Sound strange? Here's why this happens:

Only some people bother to create a "last will and testament." People who have a "last will and testament" know what will happen to their assets after they die. Everyone else has a plan crafted for them by the government.

Who do you want to decide who gets what you owned while you were alive? You, or the government?

A will is a document that provides directions on how to dispose of tangible assets that you own, when you die. You may be able to do a will yourself from a kit; on the other hand, if you have something worth leaving, you may want to get a competent attorney to create a will for you.

DOCUMENT #2: Durable Power of Attorney

A "durable power of attorney" is a document that lets someone act, on your behalf, if you are unable to do so. Best if professionally prepared, but there are good "do it yourself" documents out there. See Appendix B for a sample.

DOCUMENT #3: Living Will

A "living will" is a document that states what medical treatment you want if you are unable to clearly communicate when you need treatment. Best if professionally prepared, but there are good "do it yourself" documents out there. See Appendix B for a sample.

DOCUMENT #4: Health Care Surrogate

A health care surrogate is someone to make health care decisions for you if you cannot. You name someone to this position using a document similar to the sample in Appendix B. Best if professionally prepared, but there are good "do it yourself" documents out there. Or ask your local hospital which form they use.

These four documents are not optional. You need to have them, they need to be accessible, they need to be periodically updated, and more than one person needs to have copies. If not, other people will make decisions for you, and they may not be decisions you would have made for yourself.

Let me tell you a personal story. My Dad had aged gracefully, into his mid-80's, with a slate of known health issues that he was being treated for. But when he suffered his first heart attack, it was a surprise to all—his children and his doctors. He had done such a good job of taking care of his body—eating right, exercising, etc., that the nearly complete blockage of some of his major arteries had escaped detection because he developed a strong collateral system of blood delivery. In short, by the time anyone realized he had heart problems, repair was impossible. Surgery might have fixed the arteries, but the recovery would have killed him. We were told, eight hours after his heart failed, that he probably would not live. Over the next few days, he was unable to communicate, and we had to decide on a course of action. We had three doctors advise us—a primary care physician, and two cardiologists. One cardiologist was young, and fatalistic. She advised doing nothing, just sending him home, providing pain medication, but taking no aggressive actions that would prolong his life. She was balancing keeping him alive against a projected daily routine of doctors' offices and hospitals. She was athletic, young, and active. That type of life was an anathema to her. The older cardiologist proposed a more aggressive course of action, which would have exposed Dad to the possibility that he would spend significant amounts of time, for the rest of his life, visiting medical offices. (While you or I might not like such a routine, for Dad, who was retired, and missed seeing large numbers of people every day, being out and about, interacting with others, joking with medical staff, dining out between appointments, running into people he knew, was not a terrible life. He was used to purpose in life, and doing things—keeping appointments, working on his health—was purposeful. He would have hated wandering the shopping mall, especially since prolonged physical activity tired him out.) The primary care physician, who was just a decade younger than Dad, proposed even more treatment, keeping him alive, no matter what the quality of his life would be. Three great doctors, three different recommendations. Which one was correct? Fortunately, we knew Dad, and we knew what his wishes would be, and we proceeded accordingly. It turned out that we were right, and he lived five and a half more months, putting up with the doctor visits and hospitalizations in exchange for completing tasks he wanted to accomplish, including throwing a wedding for his last unmarried child (ten days before he died).

The point is, the doctors did not know him well, and their recommendations did not express his wishes. Their recommendations expressed their wishes for themselves—that was the only frame of reference they had. Dad was fortunate enough to have children who knew him. Had he not, since he left no directives, the treatment he received would have been what someone else wanted, and not necessarily what he would have wanted.

APPENDIX A: SPREAD SHEET FOR ASSETS, LIABILITIES, INCOME AND EXPENSES

Monthly Expenses:

Mortgage/Rent		Camp	
HOA/Condo Fees		Entertainment/Sports	
Electric		Vacation	
Water		Recreation	
Cable/Satellite radio		Medical	
Internet		Club dues	
Telephone		Holiday Expenses	
Cell Phone		Birthday celebrations	
Trash		Religious expenses/dues	
Groceries		Health club	
Dining Out		Auto Payments	
Housekeeper		Dues & Subscriptions	
Lawn		Pre-need	
Pool		Student Loan repayment	
Gas		Educational Expenses	
Home Improvements		Allowances	
Pest Control		Service Contracts	
Alarm System		Hobbies	
Laundry		Cash Spent	
Child Care		Other	
Day Care		Auto Insurance	
Pet Care/Insurance		Home Insurance	
OTC Medications/Diets		Boat Insurance	
Tutoring		Umbrella Insurance	
529 Contributions		Life Insurance	
Clothing		Medical Insurance	
Furnishings		Disability Insurance	
Charity		Totals	

Monthly Income

Income before taxes	
Take Home income	
Pay frequency/year	
Bonus	
Self-Employment Income	
Real Estate Income	
Investment Income	
SSI/SSDI	
Child Support/Alimony	
Other Income	

Liabilities

Home Equity	
Home Equity	
Home Equity	
Credit Card	
Credit Card	
Credit Card	
Credit Card	
Credit Card	
Credit Card	
Credit Card	
Credit Card	
Student loans	
Auto loans	

Assets

Checking Account	
Checking Account	
Savings Account	
Savings Account	
CD's	
CD's	
Money Market	
Money Market	
Tradtional IRA	
Tradtional IRA	
Roth IRA	
Roth IRA	
401K	
401k	
TSA/403b	
TSA/403b	
Profit Sharing	
Profit Sharing	
Investment Account	
Investment Account	
Annuity	
Annuity	
Real Estate	
Real Estate	

APPENDIX B: SAMPLE DOCUMENTS

THE ATTACHED LEGAL DOCUMENTS ARE SPECIMEN DOCUMENTS FOR INFORMATION ONLY.

Notice: These legal forms are provided for general informational purposes for reference only.
They are provided only to illustrate the common provisions of these types of documents.

<u>Berlin Consulting Group, Inc is not a law firm and we are not attorneys.</u>

Legal Information Is Not Legal Advice (the application of law to an individual's specific situation.)

Consult a lawyer to get professional assurance that any information you obtain (in this book or elsewhere), and your interpretation of it, is appropriate to your particular situation.

SAMPLE DECLARATION OF LIVING WILL

FOR _____

Declaration made this _____ day of
_____, 20____.

To my family, my physician, my health care professional, my lawyers and all others whom it may concern, I, _____, willfully and voluntarily make known my desire that my dying shall not be artificially prolonged under the circumstances set forth below, and do hereby declare:

While this document consists of two (2) parts, it is my intention that part one (1) shall be given effect, unless a court of competent jurisdiction rules the same to be ineffective. In that case, it is my intention that part two (2) which fully conforms to the existing Florida Statute be given effect.

Part I

I have fully discussed the contents of this Living Will with the individuals designated in my Designation of Health Care Surrogate. I have discussed with them my feelings and convictions concerning recourse to the modern array of technological responses to life threatening injuries and diseases, mechanical, pharmaceutical, and otherwise and, particularly, the diverse course of decline and death that I may hereafter face from currently perceived and as of yet unperceived risks and my feeling about my acceptance of death. I am satisfied that each of them cares for and loves me and sympathetically understands my views about death, and the process of death. They understand the dignity I desire in my dying. I have perfect confidence in their judgment.

In order to give concrete and practical effect to these feeling and convictions, I direct that the authority under this instrument is conferred if, whenever, for so long as I am unable to communicate decision regarding my health care. In case of doubt, my inability in this regard shall be determined solely by the individual designated and currently acting as my health care Surrogate, after said individual concludes that I am unable to make such decisions and then after consulting with any person said individual deems advisable, including without limitation any health care professional.

My health care Surrogate shall have complete authority to make all decisions regarding alleviative or curative therapy for, or maintenance of, my body or any part thereof, including care of my mental and emotional facilities, notwithstanding any real or apparent pecuniary interest that my Surrogate shall have in any property in which I have an interest and without regard to any expectant property interest that may inure to said Surrogate as a result of my death.

I authorize my Surrogate to do everything that in his or her judgment I would wish to have done if I were capable of making a decision with respect to instituting, continuing, withholding, withdrawing or terminating any treatment or procedure whatsoever, whether the procedure is commonly deemed to be intrusive and whether it is customarily prescribed in cases like mine, and irrespective of any and all risks to me of further physical, mental, or emotional injury or deterioration or death, that might attend the carrying out of such wishes. The authority under this paragraph extends specifically, but without limitation, to the providing or withholding, as my Surrogate shall, in his or her absolute discretion, determine, of forced hydration or nutrition or both. My Surrogate shall be the sole determiner of what I would wish to have done with respect to these matters.

In carrying out my wishes, my Surrogate shall take into account my preferences for a quality of life, not necessarily a quantity of life, and my preferences that I not continue to live for a prolonged period of time without reasonable prospect of amelioration or recovery (either one) in any irreversible coma or unconscious state or (2) in a conscious state with severely or irreversibly impaired cognitive faculties, massive paralysis, or with severe, uncontrollable pain or suffering, whether physical or psychological. My Surrogate shall be the sole determiner of whether the conditions referred to herein have occurred after seeking such advice as my Surrogate deems advisable.

I hereby approve and ratify everything my Surrogate does or purports to do in carrying out my intentions hereunder and give my surrogate full power and authority by this instrument as I would have, if personally able to act.

I understand and appreciate the inherent difficulty of writing in a medical context and the possibility of ambiguity between the language of this instrument and medical terminology. For example, I fully appreciate that ambiguity surrounds such medical terms as "terminal," "permanent vegetative state," and "irreversible." I also know how impossible it is for me to express specific intent with respect to a variety of medical conditions I may encounter and endure in the future. But, because of the faith and confidence I have in my Surrogate, above all others, it is my intent that he or she be the sole determiner of whether I will be allowed to die and of the meaning of this instrument.

I understand the full import of this Declaration and I am emotionally and mentally competent to make this Declaration.

PART II

If at any time I should have a terminal condition and my attending physician and a consulting physician have independently determined that there can be no recovery from such condition and that my death is imminent, where the application of life-prolonging procedures would serve only to artificially prolong the dying process, I direct that such procedures be withheld or withdrawn, and that I be permitted to die naturally with only the administration of medication or the performance of any medical procedure deemed necessary to provide me with comfort care or to alleviate pain.

I do desire that nutrition and hydration (food and water) be withheld or withdrawn when the application of such procedures would serve only to prolong artificially the process of dying.

In the absence of my ability to give directions regarding the use of such life-prolonging procedures, it is my intention that this declaration shall be honored by my family and physician as the final expression of my legal right to refuse medical or surgical treatment and accept the consequences for such refusal.

I understand the full import of this declaration and I am emotionally and mentally competent to make this declaration.

SAMPLE DURABLE POWER OF ATTORNEY
FOR _____

I, _____, as Principal (the "Principal"), residing in _____ County, Florida, have this day appointed _____, as my "Agent" to individually exercise the powers set forth below. If my Agent is unwilling or unable to serve as my "Agent", I appoint an individual personally selected by _____ to act as my "Agent" in all decisions made under this power of attorney.

My Agent(s) are authorized in their absolute discretion from time to time and at any time, with respect to any and all of my property and interest in property, real, personal, intangible and mixed, as follows:

1. Power to Sell. To sell any and every kind of property wherever located that I may own now or in the future, real, personal, intangible, and/or mixed, including homestead real property owned by me at the time of the execution of this document more specifically described in attached Exhibit "A", if any, or acquired by me after the execution of this document, including, without being limited to, contingent and expectant interests, marital rights, and any rights of survivorship incident to joint tenancy or tenancy by the entirety, upon such terms and conditions and security as my Agent shall deem appropriate and to grant options with respect to sales thereof; to make such disposition of the proceeds of such sale or sales (including expending such proceeds for my benefit) as my Agent shall deem appropriate.

2. Power to Buy. To buy every kind of property, real, personal, intangible, or mixed, including homestead real

property owned by me at the time of execution of this document or acquired by me after the execution of this document upon such terms and conditions as my Agent shall deem appropriate; to obtain options with respect to such purchases; to arrange for appropriate disposition, use, safekeeping, and/or insuring of any such property purchased by my Agent; to borrow money for the purposes described herein and to secure such borrowings in such manner as my Agent shall deem appropriate; to use any credit card held in my name to make such purchases and to sign such charge slips as may be necessary to use such credit card; to repay from any funds belonging to me any money borrowed and to pay for any purchases made or cash advances using credit cards issued to me.

3. Power to Invest. To invest and reinvest all or any part of my property in any property or interest (including undivided interests) and property, real, personal, tangible, intangible or mixed, wherever located, including without being limited to, commodities, contracts of all kinds, securities of all kinds, bonds, debentures, notes (secured and unsecured), stocks of corporations regardless of class, interest in limited partnerships, real estate or any interest in real estate whether or not productive at the time of the investment, interest in trusts, investment trusts, whether of the open, and/or closed fund types, and participation in common, collective or pooled trust funds, or annuity contracts, without being limited by any statute or rule of law concerning investments by fiduciaries; to sell and terminate any investments, whether made by me or my Agent; to establish, utilize and terminate checking, savings and money market accounts with financial institutions of all kinds; to establish, utilize and terminate accounts with securities brokers; to establish, utilize and terminate

managing agency accounts with corporate fiduciaries; to employ, utilize the services of, compensate and terminate the services of such financial and investment advisors and consultants as my Agent shall deem appropriate.

4. <u>Power to Manage Real Property.</u> With respect to real property which I own as of the date of this instrument and any real property I may hereinafter acquire or receive and my personal residence and my homestead real property, provided, however, current law authorizes said use; to lease, sublease, release; to object, remove and relieve tenants or other persons from, and recover possession of by all lawful means; to accept real property as a gift or as security for a loan; to collect, sue for, receive and receipt for rents and profits and to conserve, invest or utilize any and all such rents, profits and receipts for the purposes described in this paragraph; to do any acts of management and conservation; to pay, compromise, or to contest tax assessments and to apply for refunds therewith; to hire assistance and labor; to so divide develop, dedicate to public use without consideration, and/or dedicate easements over; to maintain, protect, repair, preserve, insure, build upon, demolish, alter or improve all or any part thereof; to release or partially release real property from a lien; to sell and to buy the same or other real property; to mortgage and/ or convey by deed of trust or otherwise encumber any real property now or hereafter owned by me, whether acquired by me or for me by my Agent.

5. <u>Power to Manage Personal Property.</u> With respect to personal property: to lease, sublease, and release; to recover possession by all lawful means; to collect, sue for, receive and receipt rents and profits there from; to maintain, protect, repair, preserve, insure, alter or

improve all or any part thereof; to sell and to buy the same or other personal property; to mortgage and/or grant security interests in any personal property or intangibles now or hereafter owned by me, whether acquired by me or for me by my Agent.

6. <u>Power to Exercise Rights and Securities.</u> To exercise all rights with respect to corporate securities which I now own or hereafter acquire, including the right to sell, grant security interest in and to buy the same or different securities; to establish, utilize and terminate brokerage accounts; to vote at all meetings of security holders, regular or special; to make such payments as my Agent deems necessary, appropriate, incidental or convenient to the owning and holding of such securities, to receive, retain, expend for benefit, invest and reinvest or make such dispositions my Agent shall deem appropriate all additional securities, cash or property (including the proceeds from the sales of my securities) to which I may be or become entitled by reason of my ownership of any security.

7. <u>Power to Demand and Receive.</u> To demand, arbitrate, settle, sue for, collect, receive, deposit, expend for my benefit, reinvest, or make such other appropriate disposition of, as my Agent deems appropriate, all cash, rights to the payment of cash, property (real, personal, tangible, intangible and/or mixed), rights and/or benefits to which I am now or may in the future become entitled, regardless of the identity of the individual or public or private entity involved (and for purposes of receiving social security benefits and other public assistance benefits) my Agent is herewith appointed my "Representative Payee"; to utilize all lawful means and

methods for such purposes; to make such compromises, release, settlements and discharges with respect thereto as my Agent shall deem appropriate.

8. <u>Power with Respect to Employment Benefits.</u> To create and contribute to an IRA or employee benefit plan for my benefit; to select any payment option under any IRA or employee benefit plan of which I am a participant, or to change options I have selected; to make and change beneficiary designations; to make voluntary contributions to such plans; to make "roll-overs" of plan benefits into other retirement plans; to borrow money and purchase assets there from and sell assets thereto, if authorized by any such plan.

9. <u>Power with Respect to Bank Accounts.</u> To establish accounts of all kinds, including checking, savings and money market, for me with financial institutions of any kind, including but not limited to, banks and thrift institutions, to modify, terminate, make deposits to and write checks on, or make withdrawals from all accounts in my name or with respect to which I am an authorized signatory (except accounts held by me in a fiduciary capacity), whether or not any such account was established by me or for me by my Agent, to negotiate, endorse or transfer any checks or other instruments with respect to any such account; to contract for services rendered by any bank or financial institution.

10. <u>Power with Respect to Safe Deposit Boxes.</u> To contract with any institution for the maintenance of a safety deposit box in my name; to have access to all safe deposit boxes in my name with respect to which I am an authorized

signatory, whether or not the contract for such safety deposit box was executed by me (either alone or jointly with others) or by my Agent in my name; to add to and remove from the contents of any such safety deposit box, including the authority to drill the box in case the keys are misplaced, and to terminate any and all contracts for such boxes.

11. <u>Power with Respect to Legal and other Actions.</u> To institute, supervise, prosecute, defend, intervene in, abandon, compromise, arbitrate, settle, dismiss and appeal from any and all legal equitable, judicial or administrative hearings, actions, suits, proceedings, attachments or arrests, involving me in any way, including but not limited to, claims by or against me arising out of property damage or personal injuries suffered by or caused by me or under such circumstances that the loss resulting there from will or may fall on me and otherwise engage in litigation involving me, my property or any interests of mine, including any property or interest or person for which or whom I have or may have any responsibility.

12. <u>Power to Borrow Money.</u> To borrow money for my account upon such terms and conditions as my Agent shall deem appropriate and to secure such borrowing by the granting of security interest in any property or interest in property which I may now or hereafter own; to borrow money upon any life insurance policies owned by me upon my life for any purpose and to grant a security interest in such policy to secure any such loan; and no insurance company shall be under any obligation whatsoever to determine the need for such loan or the application of the proceeds to my Agent.

13. <u>Power to Create, Fund, Amend and Terminate Trust Solely for the Benefit of the Principal.</u> To execute a Revocable Trust Agreement with such Trustee or Trustees as my Agent shall select, which Trust may provide that all income and principal may be paid to me, to some person for my benefit or applied for my benefit in such amounts as I or my Agent shall request or as the Trustee or Trustees shall determine, and that on my death, any remaining income and principal shall be paid pursuant to the terms of my Last Will and Testament in effect from time to time or if no such document exists, then according to Florida law, and that the Trust may be revoked or amended by me or my Agent at any time and from time to time; provided, however, that any amendment by my Agent must be such that by law or under provisions of this instrument such amendment could have been included in the original trust agreement; to deliver and convey any or all of my assets to the Trustee of the Trust itself; to add any or all of my assets to such a Trust already in existence at the time of the creation of this instrument or created by me at any time thereafter. The Trustee shall be permitted to create, amend or revoke any trust instrument fund or distribute out of trust such trust assets, which in the Trustee's sole discretion would allow me to become eligible for any government benefits, including, but not limited to the Medicaid Institutional Care Program. The Trustee may be a bank or trust company authorized to do business in the state of my domicile, the state of domicile of my Agent, or any state in which my Agent or I may from time to time or at any time reside.

14. <u>Power to Disclaim, Renounce, Release or Abandon Property Interest.</u> To renounce, disclaim any property or interest in property or powers to which, for any reason

and by any means, I may become entitled, whether by gift, testate or intestate succession, to release or abandon any property or interest in property or powers which I may now or hereafter own, including any interest in or rights over trusts (including the right to alter, amend, revoke or terminate) and to exercise any right to claim an elective share in any estate or under any will, and in exercising such discretion, my Agent may take into account such matters as shall include, but not be limited to, any reduction in estate or inheritance taxes on my estate, and the effect of such renunciation or disclaimer upon persons interested in my estate and persons who would receive the renounced or disclaimed property.

15. <u>Power with Respect to Insurance.</u> To insure my life or the life of anyone in whom I have an insurable interest; to continue life insurance policies now or hereafter owned by me on either my life or the lives of others; to pay all insurance premiums; to select any options under such policies; to increase coverage under such policies; to borrow against any such policy; to pursue all insurance claims on my behalf; to purchase and/or maintain and pay all premiums for medical insurance covering me, and any person I am obligated or may have assumed the obligation to support; to carry insurance of such kind and in such amounts as my Agent shall deem appropriate to protect my assets against hazard and to protect me from any liability; to pay the premiums therefore; to pursue claims there under; to designate and change beneficiaries of insurance policies insuring my life and beneficiaries under any annuity contract in which I might have an interest; to decrease coverage under or cancel any of the policies described herein; to receive and make such

disposition of the cash value upon termination of any such policy as my Agent shall deem appropriate.

16. <u>Power with Respect to Taxes.</u> To represent me in all matters; to prepare, sign, and file federal, state and local income, gift and other tax returns of all kinds, including joint returns, FICA returns, payroll tax returns, claims for refunds, requests for extensions of time, petitions to the tax court or other courts regarding tax matters, and any and all other tax related documents; to pay taxes due, collect and make such disposition of refunds as my Agent shall deem appropriate, post bonds, receive confidential information in contested and uncontested matters involving the IRS and/or any state and/or local taxing authority; to exercise any elections I may have under federal state or local tax laws; and generally to represent me or obtain professional representation of me in all matters and proceedings of all kinds for all periods between the years 1970 and 2030 before all officers of the Internal Revenue Service and state and local authorities including but not limited to forms 1040, 709, 2848; to engage, compensate and discharge attorneys, accountants, and other tax and financial advisors and consultants to represent or assist me in connection with any and all tax matters involving or in any way related to me or any property in which I have or may have any interest or responsibility.

17. <u>Power to Make Gifts.</u> To make gifts, grants or other transfers without consideration either outright or in trust (including the forgiveness of indebtedness and the completion of any charitable pledges I may have made) to such person or organizations as my Agent shall select; to consent to the splitting of gifts under Section 2513 of the

Internal Revenue Code and any successor sections thereto or similar provisions of any state of local gift tax law; to pay any gift tax that may arise by reason of such gift; provided, however, that my Agent not make any gifts constituting a future interest within the meaning of the IRS Code.

18. <u>Power with Respect to Collecting Government Entitlements.</u> To collect amounts due to the principal and qualify the principal for various government entitlements such as Medicaid or Supplemental Social Security, including the power to renounce or disclaim an inheritance and/or insurance proceeds, to divest me of sufficient assets to qualify for medical assistance or to convert my assets into assets to be owned by me which are exempt from the resources allowable under the Medicaid rules and regulations, and to change my domicile to another state where the Medicaid eligibility rules are more favorable.

19. <u>Power to Transfer Assets to Qualify for Government Benefits.</u> To transfer every kind of property, real, personal, tangible, intangible or mixed, including homestead real property, so that I might be eligible for any programs of public benefit, including but not limited to, Supplemental Social Security (SSI), Federal Social Security Disability Insurance (SSDI), Medicaid (or state equivalent), state insurance, Florida Supplemental Income Program (FSIP), Old Age Survivor and Disability Insurance Program (OASDI) and Aid in Attendance from the Veteran's Administration.

20. <u>Power to Provide Support to Others.</u> To support and/ or continue to support any person whom I have taken to support or to whom I may owe an obligation of support

in the same manner and in accordance with the same standard of living as I may have provided in the past (adjusted if necessary by circumstances due to inflation), including but not limited to the payment of real property taxes, payment on loans secured by my residence, maintenance of my residence, food, clothing and shelter, medical, dental and psychiatric care, normal vacations and travel expenses and education.

21. <u>Power to Make Loans.</u> To lend money and property at such interest rate, if any, and upon such terms and conditions, and with such security, if any, as my Agent may deem appropriate; to renew, extend and modify any such loan or loans I have previously made; to guarantee the obligations of any such person; to consent to the renewal extension and modification of such obligation; provided, however, that my Agent shall not lend my money or property to my Agent, but this provision shall not apply to prior loans made by me to my Agent.

22. <u>Power to Hire and Fire.</u> To employ, compensate and discharge such domestic, medical, and professional personnel including lawyers, accountants, doctors, nurses, brokers, financial consultants, advisors, companions, servants and employees, as my Agent deems appropriate.

23. <u>Power to Sign Documents.</u> To execute, endorse, seal acknowledge, deliver and file or record agreements, instruments, conveyances of real (including homestead real property pursuant to state law) and personal property, instruments granting and perfecting security instruments and obligations, orders for the payment of money, receipts, releases, waivers, elections, vouchers, consents, satisfactions and certificates.

24. <u>Power to Borrow, Spend, Liquidate and Secure.</u> To expend my funds and to liquidate my property or to borrow money in order to produce such funds and to secure any such borrowings with security interest in any property, real, personal, or intangible that I may now or hereafter own.

25. <u>Power to do Miscellaneous Acts.</u> To open, read, respond to and redirect my mail; to represent me before the U.S. Postal Service in all matters relating to mail service; to establish, cancel continue or initiate my membership in organizations and associations of all kinds; to take and give or deny custody of all my important documents, including but not limited to, my will, codicils, trust agreements, deeds, leases, life insurance policies, contracts and securities and to disclose or refuse to disclose such documents; to obtain and release or deny information or records of all kinds relating to me, any interest of mine or to any person for whom I am responsible.

26. <u>Agent has Power to Act Alone.</u> The powers conferred on my Agent or in the case of my successor co-agents acting jointly by this instrument may be exercised by my Agent(s) alone and my Agent's signature(s) or act(s) under the authority granted in this instrument may be accepted by Persons as fully authorized by me and with the same force and effect as if I were personally present and acting on my own behalf. Consequently, all acts lawfully done by my Agent(s) hereunder are done with my consent and have the same validity and effect as if I were personally present and personally exercise the powers myself and it shall inure to the benefit of and bind me and my heirs, assigns and personal representatives.

27. Third Party Reliance

(a) Any third party may rely upon the authority granted in my Durable Power of Attorney until the third party has received notice as provided herein.

(b) Until a third party has received notice of revocation pursuant to the terms contained herein, partial or complete termination of the Durable Power of Attorney by adjudication of incapacity, my death, or the occurrence of an event referenced in this Durable Power of Attorney, the third party may act in reliance upon the authority granted in this Durable Power of Attorney.

(c) A third party that has not received written notice hereunder may, but need   not, require that my attorney in fact execute an affidavit stating that there has been no revocation, partial or complete termination, or suspension of the Durable Power of Attorney at the time the Power of Attorney is exercised. A written affidavit executed by my attorney in fact under this paragraph may, but need not, be in the following form:

(d) Third parties who act in reliance upon the authority granted to my attorney in fact hereunder and in accordance with the instructions of the attorney in fact will be held harmless by me from any loss suffered or liability incurred as a result of actions taken prior to receipt of written notice of revocation, suspension, notice of a petition to determine incapacity, partial or complete termination, or in my death. A person who acts in good faith upon any representation, direction, decision or act of my attorney in fact is not liable to me or to my estate, beneficiaries or joint owners for those acts.

(e) My attorney in fact is not liable for any acts or decisions made by him or her in good faith and under the terms of the Durable Power of Attorney.

28. <u>Authorization to Release Information to Agent.</u> All persons from whom my Agent may request information regarding me, my personal or financial affairs, or any information which I am entitled to receive are hereby authorized to provide such information to my Agent without limitation and are released from any legal liability whatsoever to me, my estate, my heirs and assigns for complying with my Agent's request.

29. <u>Durability Provision.</u> This instrument is to be construed and interpreted as a Durable Power of Attorney. This Durable Power of Attorney shall not be affected by disability of the Principal except as provided by statute. The enumeration of specific items, rights, and acts, or powers herein is not intended to, nor does it limit or restrict, and is not to be construed or interpreted as limiting or restricting, the general powers herein granted to said Agent.

30. <u>Reimbursement of Agent.</u> My Agent shall be entitled to reimbursement for all reasonable costs and expenses actually incurred and paid by my Agent on my behalf under any provision of this instrument; and, in addition, my agent shall be paid for services rendered to me at a reasonable hourly rate of service, in accordance with written records created, maintained and preserved by my Agent.

31. <u>Nomination of Agent as Guardian for Principal.</u> To the extent that I am permitted by law to do so, I herewith nominate, constitute and appoint my Agent to serve as my guardian of my property, or in any similar representative capacity.

32. <u>Severability.</u> If any part of any provision of this instrument shall become invalid and unenforceable under applicable law, such part shall be ineffective to the extent of such invalidity only, without in any way affecting the remaining parts of such provision or the remaining provisions of this instrument.

33. <u>Governing Law.</u> This instrument shall be governed by the laws of the State of Florida in all respects, including its validity, construction, interpretation and termination, and to the extent permitted by law shall be applicable to all property of mine, real, personal, tangible, intangible, or mixed, wherever and in whatever state of the United States or foreign country the site of such property is at any time located and whether any such property is now owned by me or hereafter acquired by me or for me by my Agent.

34. <u>Revocation, Removal, Amendment and Resignation.</u> This instrument may be amended or revoked by me, and I may remove my Agent at any time by the execution by me of a written instrument of revocation, amendment, or removal delivered to my Agent. If this instrument has been recorded in the public records, the instrument of revocation, amendment or removal shall be filed or recorded in the same public records. My Agent may resign by the execution of a written resignation delivered to me, or if I am incapacitated, by delivery to any person with whom I am residing or who has care and custody of me.

35. <u>Effective Date.</u> The rights, powers and authority of said Agent herein granted shall commence and be in full force and effect on the date of execution of this Durable Power of Attorney and such rights, powers and authority shall remain in full force and effect thereafter until revoked by written notice.

36. <u>Notification.</u> Pursuant to state law my Agent, has received notification of the execution of this Durable Power of Attorney and the acknowledgment of said notice is evidenced by his execution of the attached Receipt.

SAMPLE DESIGNATION OF HEALTH CARE SURROGATE
FOR _____

1. DESIGNATION OF HEALTH CARE SURROGATE.

I, _____, hereby appoint, in order of preference and succession, as my Surrogate to make health and personal care decisions for me as authorized in this document and pursuant to Florida Statute, the following:

1. _____, my _____, to serve.

2. If _____ is unavailable or unwilling to serve to act in this capacity, I appoint _____ to act as my successor surrogate decision maker, with the power to act on my behalf.

2. EFFECTIVE DATE AND DURABILITY.

By this document I intend to designate a health care surrogate effective upon, and only during, any period of incapacity in which, in the opinion of my Surrogate and attending physician, I am unable to make or communicate a choice regarding a particular health care decision. This designation of surrogacy for health care shall not be affected by my disability except as provided by Statute.

3. SURROGATE'S POWERS.

I grant to my Surrogate full authority to make decisions for me regarding my health care. In exercising this authority, my Surrogate shall follow my desires as stated in this document or otherwise known to my Surrogate. In making any decision, my Surrogate shall attempt to discuss the proposed decision with me to determine my desires if I am able to communicate in any way. If my Surrogate cannot determine the choice I would want made, then my Surrogate shall make a choice for me based upon what my Surrogate believes to be in my best interests. My Surrogate's authority to interpret my desires is intended to be as broad as possible. Accordingly, my Surrogate is authorized as follows:

A. To consent, refuse, or withdraw consent to any and all types of medical care, treatment, surgical, diagnostic procedures, medication, and the use of mechanical or other procedures that affect any bodily function, including (but not limited to) artificial respiration, nutritional support and hydration, and cardiopulmonary resuscitation;

B. To have access to medical records and information to the same extent that I am entitled to, including the right to disclose the contents to others;

C. To authorize my admission to or discharge (even against medical advice) from any hospital, nursing home, residential care, assisted living or similar facility or service;

D. To contract on my behalf for any health care related service or facility on my behalf, without my Surrogate incurring personal financial liability for such contracts;

E. To retain and dismiss medical, social service, and other support personnel responsible for my care;

F. To authorize, or refuse to authorize, any medication or procedure, intended to relieve pain, even though such use may lead to physical damage, addiction or hasten the moment of (but not intentionally cause) my death;

G. To make anatomical gifts of part or all of my body for medical purposes, authorize an autopsy, and direct the disposition of my remains, to the extent permitted by law.

H. To apply for public benefits, such as Medicare and Medicaid, and to have access to information regarding my income and assets to the extent required to make said application;

I. To take any other action necessary to do what I authorize here (but not limited to) granting any waiver or release from liability required by any hospital, physician, or other health care provider, signing any documents relating to refusals of treatment or the leaving of a facility against medical advice, and pursuing any legal action in my name, and at the expense of my estate to force compliance with my wishes as determined by my Surrogate, or to seek actual or punitive damages for the failure to comply.

4. LIVING WILL.

With respect to any Life-Sustaining Treatment, I have executed a "Living Will", a copy of which is attached hereto. I direct my Surrogate to follow said "Living Will". My "Living Will" states that nutrition and hydration are to be withheld or withdrawn and I direct my Surrogate to follow my instructions.

5. APPOINTMENT OF GUARDIAN.

If a court appoints a guardian of my estate or other fiduciary of my property, my Surrogate shall continue to make health care decisions, unless the court specifically removes such power. In the event that I become incapacitated such that a court of competent jurisdiction determines that a guardian of my person needs to be appointed, then I request that the individuals named herein, in order of preference, be appointed as such guardian of my person.

6. RESTRICTIONS.

Pursuant to Florida law, my Surrogate is not authorized to provide consent for sterilization, electroshock therapy, psychosurgery, and experimental treatments through therapy or admission to a mental health facility.

7. PROTECTION OF THIRD PARTIES WHO RELY ON MY SURROGATE.

No person who relies in good faith, upon any representations by my Surrogate or Successor Surrogate shall be liable to me, my estate, my heirs or assigns, for recognizing the Surrogate's authority, so long as my Surrogate is acting as a reasonably prudent person should act in accordance with the instructions herein.

8. RELIANCE.

My health care Surrogate and all health care providers and facilities shall be entitled to rely upon this Designation of Health Care Surrogate until such person or facility receives actual knowledge or actual notice of the revocation of this Designation of Health Care Surrogate by a subsequent writing.

9. INDEMNITY.

My estate shall hold harmless and indemnify my health care Surrogate from all liability for acts done in good faith on my behalf pursuant to this Designation of Health Care Surrogate.

10. PRIVACY.

My Surrogate shall have the power to exercise in all respects any right of my privacy, my right to be left alone, and my right to be free of unwanted medical treatment, and to waive any and all privileges arising out of any confidential relationship and to exercise and assert any rights to privilege in connection with disclosure of information to others.

11. ADMINISTRATIVE PROVISIONS.
    A. The execution by me of this document revokes any prior designation of a health care surrogate.
    B. The execution by me of a written revocation of this Designation of Health Care Surrogate shall revoke the same.
    C. The execution by me of another Designation of Health Care Surrogate after the date I have executed this Designation of Health Care Surrogate shall revoke the prior Designation.
    D. This Designation of Health Care Surrogate is intended to be valid in any jurisdiction in which it is presented.
    E. My Surrogate shall not be entitled to compensation for services performed hereunder, but he or she shall be entitled to reimbursement for all reasonable expenses incurred as a result of carrying out any provision hereof.
    F. The powers delegated hereunder are separable, so that the invalidity of one or more powers shall not affect any others.

ABOUT THE AUTHOR:

I was born in 1953, the first child of Lila and George Berlin, and lived in a tiny apartment in Manhattan for six months, until my father bought a $15,000, 2 bedroom, 1 bath starter home in the suburbs. Mom worked as a nurse until I was born, and then retired to take care of what would quickly become a family of four. Dad, a Navy vet and a college trained civil engineer, began a 15 year career in a concrete supply company, thinking he would be there forever. Growing up, I often spent weekends with Dad, hosing the chutes of concrete trucks before the tailings could harden. After the concrete company went bankrupt, and the owners forged papers saying that Dad had an ownership position so as to try to saddle him with their liabilities, I figured out that financial security lay not with working for others, but in building something of my own.

Mom's youth had been colored by the Depression. Her father was often out of work, and her mother struggled to provide for the four girls. As a teenager, she sold sandwiches by the roadside, near a farm that relatives lived on for a while, and then, back in Manhattan, went door to door selling subscriptions. The fear of not having food or money became ingrained into her subconscious, and I clearly remember bringing a sack lunch to school, every day, with 3 pennies to buy a half-pint of milk. Rarely was there an extra nickel for a candy bar, although an extra nickel a day, $13 a year, would not have taxed the family budget (even if all four children got that nickel). A cafeteria hot lunch for thirty-five cents was achieved but once or twice a year. Suffice to say, with the school lunch program being my Holy Grail of gourmet food, the first time I went to an "all you can eat" buffet, I thought I had died and gone to Heaven. (God only knows what damage I have inflicted on my children by making them eat what was in the refrigerator, irrespective of its age or state of decay.)

The lesson I learned from vicariously living Mom's youth was that if I did not provide for myself, I might, indeed go hungry in the future.

I began my working career in 3rd grade, publishing a short-lived, one page community newspaper, which Mrs. Shepard, my teacher, was gracious enough to make mimeo copies of at school. I attempted to peddle these door to door for 3 cents a copy, but the smell of the acetone toner brought back too many memories of surprise quizzes and worksheets that my potential customers had endured in childhood, and it did not sell.

Since then, I've been involved in over 30 businesses, sometimes as an employee, but more often as owner and entrepreneur, generally with a partner, and the success or failure of my efforts dependent mainly on my wits, determination, incredibly long work day, fear of failure, and luck. These forty-plus years of adult working life have brought me a wealth of experience and insight into human behavior, and clear understanding of what it takes to succeed. It has also taught me just how ill-prepared we all are for a life of financial peace of mind. Too much is invested in hopes and dreams, and wishing things to turn out a certain way, at the expense of realistic planning.

A number of years ago, I turned to the world of insurance and finance, in part because, amidst the joys of life, several unpleasant surprises and tragic events occurred:

- My mother-in-law spent 27 years flat on her back in a nursing home, supported by Medicaid. Several State employees began their careers in the Department of

Family Services with Jane's case already open, and they retired before it was closed. She may well have been the longest case on record.

- My sister-in-law, age 61, was hit by a car, thrown 25 feet, broke everything, was in a coma for 3 months, and was still in rehab over 18 months later. She had no disability or long-term care insurance.

- My Dad passed away. He was woefully under-insured, and some of the insurance he had was totally inappropriate.

- My Mom's long-term care insurance lapsed, leaving her with annual costs in excess of $100,000.

- Some investments I had were tied to the stock market, which tanked just when I needed the money.

- It turned out that some wildly popular insurance products that I owned were invested in the stock market as well.

- I discovered that I had become middle-aged, which was quite a surprise, because I had been thinking that I was still young.

Reviewing insurance was never on my list of top 10 things to do. I did not like shopping for insurance. And I thought growing old was something that would happen in the future. But after I reviewed my policies a while ago, I concluded that I was missing important coverage, that I was paying for policies that were no longer right for me, and not getting the most out of the good policies that I owned. So I took matters into my own hand; I went to school and got a license to sell insurance. Then, I fixed my policies that were worth saving, cancelled others, and added some new ones that I needed. It occurred to me that I might not be alone, so I started talking to people. It turns out that I was right–I have yet to find anyone who likes shopping for insurance, and I've collected a set of insurance horror stories. I turned what I learned into a career—and you can save time and money and benefit from my learning, just by talking to me.

I approach insurance the way I approach everything else—studying, gaining knowledge, seeking out mentors with experience and the proper connections. And I listen to people's needs. That's what I was taught at Princeton University, and at the Wharton School of Finance, while studying for my MBA . (It's also what I taught my undergraduates students there, while I was getting my MBA.) It's the methodology I've used to build several successful businesses. It's the bedrock of my ability to help people achieve financial peace of mind.

I'd like to also mention that I have 5 wonderful children, and a fantastic wife, Nancy, without whom this book would not have been possible. We are partners in Berlin Consulting Group, and she is my best advisor and supporter. Her gentle hand in editing is found throughout this book. We look forward to the rest of middle age, and beyond, sharing what we have learned with others, in both the financial arena, and in raising children to be successful adults. You are welcome to visit our website, www.BerlinConsultingGroup.com, to learn more about the entire range of work Nancy and I do, and www.InsuranceForEnhancedLiving.com to read more about achieving financial peace of mind.